11/03

Meramec Library
St. Louis Community College
11333 Big Bend Blvd.
Kirkwood, MO 63122-5799
314-984-7797

WITHDRAWN

St. Louis Community College
at Meramec
Library

St. Louis Community College
at Meramec
Library

Bloom's BioCritiques

Dante Alighieri
Maya Angelou
Jane Austen
The Brontë Sisters
Lord Byron
Geoffrey Chaucer
Anton Chekhov
Joseph Conrad
Stephen Crane
Charles Dickens
Emily Dickinson
William Faulkner
F. Scott Fitzgerald
Robert Frost
Ernest Hemingway
Langston Hughes
Zora Neale Hurston
Stephen King
Arthur Miller
John Milton
Toni Morrison
Edgar Allan Poe
J.D. Salinger
William Shakespeare
John Steinbeck
Henry David Thoreau
Mark Twain
Alice Walker
Walt Whitman
Tennessee Williams

Bloom's BioCritiques

LORD BYRON

Edited and with an introduction by
Harold Bloom
Sterling Professor of the Humanities
Yale University

CHELSEA HOUSE
PUBLISHERS
A Haights Cross Communications Company

Philadelphia

©2004 by Chelsea House Publishers, a subsidiary of
Haights Cross Communications.

A Haights Cross Communications Company

Introduction © 2004 by Harold Bloom.

All rights reserved. No part of this publication may be
reproduced or transmitted in any form or by any means
without the written permission of the publisher.

Printed and bound in the United States of America.

10 9 8 7 6 5 4 3 2 1

Library of Congress Cataloging-in-Publication Data

Lord Byron / edited and with an introduction by Harold Bloom.
    p. cm. — (Bloom's biocritiques)
Includes bibliographical references (p.) and index.
  ISBN 0-7910-6367-4
  1. Byron, George Gordon Byron, Baron, 1788-1824—Criticism and
interpretation. I. Bloom, Harold. II. Title. III. Series.
  PR4388.L67 2003
  821'.7—dc21
                                        2003011833

Chelsea House Publishers
1974 Sproul Road, Suite 400
Broomall, PA 19008-0914

http://www.chelseahouse.com

Contributing editor: Duke Pesta

Cover design by Keith Trego

Cover: © Hulton-Deutsch Collection/CORBIS

Layout by EJB Publishing Services

CONTENTS

User's Guide   vii

The Work in the Writer   ix
    Harold Bloom

Introduction   1
    Harold Bloom

Biography of Lord Byron   5
    Karen Willis

"Darkness Visible": Byron and the Romantic Anti-Hero   59
    Duke Pesta

Hebrew Melodies and Other Lyrics of 1814–1816   85
    Robert F. Gleckner

The Book of Byron and the Book of a World   107
    Jerome J. McGann

Byron, Byronism and Byromaniacs   131
    Frances Wilson

Chronology   155

Works by Lord Byron   159

Works about Lord Byron   161

Contributors   165

Index   167

USER'S GUIDE

These volumes are designed to introduce the reader to the life and work of the world's literary masters. Each volume begins with Harold Bloom's essay "The Work in the Writer" and a volume-specific introduction also written by Professor Bloom. Following these unique introductions is an engaging biography that discusses the major life events and important literary accomplishments of the author under consideration.

Furthermore, each volume includes an original critique that not only traces the themes, symbols, and ideas apparent in the author's works, but strives to put those works into a cultural and historical perspective. In addition to the original critique is a brief selection of significant critical essays previously published on the author and his or her works followed by a concise and informative chronology of the writer's life. Finally, each volume concludes with a bibliography of the writer's works, a list of additional readings, and an index of important themes and ideas.

HAROLD BLOOM

The Work in the Writer

Literary biography found its masterpiece in James Boswell's *Life of Samuel Johnson*. Boswell, when he treated Johnson's writings, implicitly commented upon Johnson as found in his work, even as in the great critic's life. Modern instances of literary biography, such as Richard Ellmann's lives of W. B. Yeats, James Joyce, and Oscar Wilde, essentially follow in Boswell's pattern.

That the writer somehow is in the work, we need not doubt, though with William Shakespeare, writer-of-writers, we almost always need to rely upon pure surmise. The exquisite rancidities of the Problem Plays or Dark Comedies seem to express an extraordinary estrangement of Shakespeare from himself. When we read or attend *Troilus and Cressida* and *Measure for Measure*, we may be startled by particular speeches of Ulysses in the first play, or of Vincentio in the second. These speeches, of Ulysses upon hierarchy or upon time, or of Duke Vincentio upon death, are too strong either for their contexts or for the characters of their speakers. The same phenomenon occurs with Parolles, the military impostor of *All's Well That Ends Well*. Utterly disgraced, he nevertheless affirms: "Simply the thing I am/Shall make me live."

In Shakespeare, more even than in his peers, Dante and Cervantes, meaning always starts itself again through excess or overflow. The strongest of Shakespeare's creatures—Falstaff, Hamlet, Iago, Lear, Cleopatra—have an exuberance that is fiercer than their plays can contain. If Ben Jonson was at all correct in his complaint that "Shakespeare wanted art," it could have been only in a sense that he may not have intended. Where do the personalities of Falstaff or Hamlet touch a limit? What was it in Shakespeare that made the two parts of *Henry IV* and *Hamlet* into "plays unlimited"? Neither Falstaff nor Hamlet will be stopped: their wit, their beautiful, laughing speech, their intensity of being—all these are virtually infinite.

In what ways do Falstaff and Hamlet manifest the writer in the work? Evidently, we can never know, or know enough to answer with any authority. But what would happen if we reversed the question, and asked: How did the work form the writer, Shakespeare?

Of Shakespeare's inwardness, his biography tells us nothing. And yet, to an astonishing extent, Shakespeare created our inwardness. At the least, we can speculate that Shakespeare so lived his life as to conceal the depths of his nature, particularly as he rather prematurely aged. We do not have Shakespeare on Shakespeare, as any good reader of the Sonnets comes to realize: they do not constitute a key that unlocks his heart. No sequence of sonnets could be less confessional or more powerfully detached from the poet's self.

The German poet and universal genius, Goethe, affords a superb contrast to Shakespeare. Of Goethe's life, we know more than everything; I wonder sometimes if we know as much about Napoleon or Freud or any other human being who ever has lived, as we know about Goethe. Everywhere, we can find Goethe in his work, so much so that Goethe seems to crowd the writing out, just as Byron and Oscar Wilde seem to usurp their own literary accomplishments. Goethe, cunning beyond measure, nevertheless invested a rival exuberance in his greatest works that could match his personal charisma. The sublime outrageousness of the Second Part of *Faust*, or of the greater lyric and meditative poems, form a Counter-Sublime to Goethe's own daemonic intensity.

Goethe was fascinated by the daemonic in himself; we can doubt that Shakespeare had any such interests. Evidently, Shakespeare abandoned his acting career just before he composed *Measure for Measure* and *Othello*. I surmise that the egregious interventions by Vincentio and Iago displace the actor's energies into a new kind of mischief-making, a fresh opening to a subtler playwriting-within-the-play.

But what had opened Shakespeare to this new awareness? The answer is the work in the writer, *Hamlet* in Shakespeare. One can go further: it was not so much the play, *Hamlet*, as the character Hamlet, who changed Shakespeare's art forever.

Hamlet's personality is so large and varied that it rivals Goethe's own. Ironically Goethe's Faust, his Hamlet, has no personality at all, and is as colorless as Shakespeare himself seems to have chosen to be. Yet nothing could be more colorful than the Second Part of *Faust*, which is peopled by an astonishing array of monsters, grotesque devils, and classical ghosts.

A contrast between Shakespeare and Goethe demonstrates that in each—but in very different ways—we can better find the work in the person, than we can discover that banal entity, the person in the work. Goethe to many of his contemporaries, seemed to be a mortal god. Shakespeare, so far as we know, seemed an affable, rather ordinary fellow, who aged early and became somewhat withdrawn. Yet Faust, though Mephistopheles battles for his soul, is hardly worth the trouble unless you take him as an idea and not as a person. Hamlet is nearly every-idea-in-one, but he is precisely a personality and a person.

Would Hamlet be so astonishingly persuasive if his father's ghost did not haunt him? Falstaff is more alive than Prince Hal, who says that the devil haunts him in the shape of an old fat man. Three years before composing the final *Hamlet*, Shakespeare invented Falstaff, who then never ceased to haunt his creator. Falstaff and Hamlet may be said to best represent the work in the writer, because their influence upon Shakespeare was prodigious. W.H. Auden accurately observed that Falstaff possesses infinite energy: never tired, never bored, and absolutely both witty and happy until Hal's rejection destroys him. Hamlet too has infinite energy, but in him it is more curse than blessing.

Falstaff and Hamlet can be said to occupy the roles in Shakespeare's invented world that Sancho Panza and Don Quixote possess in Cervantes's. Shakespeare's plays from 1610 on (starting with *Twelfth Night*) are thus analogous to the Second Part of Cervantes's epic novel. Sancho and the Don overtly jostle Cervantes for authorship in the Second Part, even as Cervantes battles against the impostor who has pirated a continuation of his work. As a dramatist, Shakespeare manifests the work in the writer more indirectly. Falstaff's prose genius is revived in the scapegoating of Malvolio by Maria and Sir Toby Belch, while Falstaff's darker insights are developed by Feste's melancholic wit. Hamlet's intellectual resourcefulness, already deadly, becomes poisonous in Iago and in Edmund. Yet we have not crossed into the deeper abysses of the work in the writer in later Shakespeare.

No fictive character, before or since, is Falstaff's equal in self-trust. Sir John, whose delight in himself is contagious, has total confidence both in his self-awareness and in the resources of his language. Hamlet, whose self is as strong, and whose language is as copious, nevertheless distrusts both the self and language. Later Shakespeare is, as it were, much under the influence both of Falstaff and of Hamlet, but they tug him in opposite directions. Shakespeare's own copiousness of language is well-nigh incredible: a vocabulary in excess of twenty-one thousand words, almost eighteen hundred of which he coined himself. And of his word-hoard, nearly half are used only once each, as though the perfect setting for each had been found, and need not be repeated. Love for language and faith in language are Falstaffian attributes. Hamlet will darken both that love and that faith in Shakespeare, and perhaps the Sonnets can best be read as Falstaff and Hamlet counterpointing against one another.

Can we surmise how aware Shakespeare was of Falstaff and Hamlet, once they had played themselves into existence? *Henry IV, Part I* appeared in six quarto editions during Shakespeare's lifetime; *Hamlet* possibly had four. Falstaff and Hamlet were played again and again at the Globe, but Shakespeare knew also that they were being read, and he must have had contact with some of those readers. What would it have been like to discuss Falstaff or Hamlet with one of their early readers (presumably also part of their audience at the Globe), if you were the creator of such demiurges? The question would seem nonsensical to most Shakespeare scholars, but then these days they tend to be either ideologues or moldy figs. How can we recover the uncanniness of Falstaff and of Hamlet, when they now have become so familiar?

A writer's influence upon himself is an unexplored problem in criticism, but such an influence is never free from anxieties. The biocritical problem (which this series attempts to explore) can be divided into two areas, difficult to disengage fully. Accomplished works affect the author's life, and also affect her subsequent writings. It is simpler for me to surmise the effect of *Mrs. Dalloway* and *To the Lighthouse* upon Woolf's late *Between the Acts*, than it is to relate Clarissa Dalloway's suicide and Lily Briscoe's capable endurance in art to the tragic death and complex life of Virginia Woolf.

There are writers whose lives were so vivid that they seem sometimes to obscure the literary achievement: Byron, Wilde, Malraux, Hemingway. But most major Western writers do not live that exuberantly, and the greatest of all, Shakespeare, sometimes appears to have adopted the personal mask of colorlessness. And yet there are heroes of literature who struggled titanically with their own eras—Tolstoy, Milton, Victor Hugo—who nevertheless matter more for their works than their lives.

There are great figures—Emily Dickinson, Wallace Stevens, Willa Cather—who seem to have had so little of the full intensity of life when compared to the vitality of their work, that we might almost speak of the work in the work, rather than even of the work in a person. Emily Brontë might well be the extreme instance of such a visionary, surpassing William Blake in that one regard.

I conclude this general introduction to a series of literary bio-critiques by stating a tentative formula or principle for gauging the many ways in which the work influences the person and her subsequent, later work. Our influence upon ourselves is always related to the Shakespearean invention of self-overhearing, which I have written about in several other contexts. Life, as well as poetry and prose, is overheard rather than simply heard. The writer listens to herself as though she were somebody else, and the will to change begins to operate. The forces that live in us include the prior work we have done, and the dreams and waking visions that evade our dismissals.

HAROLD BLOOM

Introduction

George Gordon, Lord Byron, is literature's most notorious instance of a writer's life becoming his work, indeed taking the place of it. The illustrious Goethe is something of a rival instance, and later examples include Oscar Wilde, Ernest Hemingway, and Norman Mailer. To endeavor to speak of the work in the writer in regard to Byron is therefore a considerable challenge, which I will take up here, though on a modest scale.

Byron was a cinema idol two centuries before there was a cinema, and a rock star similar centuries before rhythm-and-blues metamorphosed into rock-and-roll. Valentino and Elvis lag in the Byronic wake, as any other popular luminary would have to run well behind the noble Lord Byron: great poet, gallant martyr to Greek independence from the Turks, reformist British politician, and an authentic anthology of every sexual possibility: incestuous heterosexuality, sodomizing of male and female, Satanic sado-masochism, pederasty, and whatever else nature makes available (with perhaps a restraint or two).

Externally, Byron's work strongly affected his life with the publication of *Childe Harold's Pilgrimage*, Cantos I and II, in 1812, when the twenty-four-year-old poet "awoke one morning and found myself famous." But that is hardly a matter of the work in a writer, except that Byron's *persona* or mask as Romantic adventurer never left him after that. It was not a question of following the big wars, like the Byronic Hemingway, nor even of achieving authentic disgust with the

1

limits of sexual experience. Instead, there was the impossible quest somehow to reconcile personal idealism and the demands of celebrity, probably the ultimate instance of celebrity ever, in the long cavalcade from Cleopatra in the ancient world down (very much down) to the present.

Everything crucial about Byron is an enigma, simultaneously ambiguous and ambivalent. The best of him emerged in his long, complex friendship with Shelley, a kind of a brother in poetic greatness, aristocratic ambivalence, and revolutionary temperament, but hardly a double or twin. Byron, according to the flamboyant Trelawny, wished to save Shelley's skull from the funeral-pyre, but Trelawny would not consent, saying he feared Byron was capable of using it as a drinking-cup. And yet Byron said to his London friends that they were all wrong about Shelley, who made everyone else seem a beast, in comparison.

Shelley, a superb critic, uniquely saw and said that Byron's *Don Juan* was the great poem of the Romantic Age, surpassing even Goethe and Wordsworth. It depends upon perspective, to some degree, but time seems to have agreed with Shelley. Certainly, the effect of *Don Juan* upon Byron himself was extraordinary. At last, the work became the life.

William Hazlitt found throughout Byron's poetry the story of "a mind preying upon itself." That can be phrased, more generously, as the record of a mind influencing itself. Byron exuberantly said of *Don Juan*: "It may be profligate but is it not *life*, is it not *the thing*?"

Indeed it is the celebrated *thing-in-itself*, the reality for which we all of us search. Its protagonist, the amiable but passive Juan, decidedly is *not* Byron. Rather, the great voice narrating the poem is more than Lord Byron's, the voice *is* Byron himself, in all his diversity and self-contradictions, an identity larger than that of the noble Lord. George Wilson Knight brilliantly remarks that, in *Don Juan*, Byron and the ocean became one, as if to resolve the poet's simultaneous faith both in nature and in eternity. I think of Hart Carne invoking the Caribbean as "this great wink of Eternity" in *Voyager II*, and reflect at the closeness of sexual dynamics in Byron and in Hart Crane.

Northrup Frye remarks that Byron, unlike his public, was not enthralled by the Byronic Hero. Since that Hero reappeared, in the next generation, in Charlotte Brontë's Rochester and Emily Brontë's Heathcliff, and lived on in Hemingway's bullfighters, big-game hunters, and heroically literate soldiers, Byron had no way of stopping what he had begun. He might have blanched at many of our current female Byrons, who have a charming way of turning into vampires.

Byron's chief debt to *Don Juan* was that it turned him inexorably to revolutionary action, perhaps because he needed to demonstrate that he was *not* Don Juan. The first two cantos of *Don Juan* were published in July, 1819. A year later, Byron joined the Carbonari in their revolution against Austrian rule. The Carbonari were defeated but in 1823, Byron and Trelawny were exiled to Greece, where "the Trumpet Voice of Liberty" died a hero's death at Missolonghi on April 19, 1824. After that, his life and work fused forever. It is good to remember however the essential Byron, who scribbled this fragment on the back of his manuscript of *Don Juan*, Canto I:

> I would to heaven that I were so much clay,
>   As I am blood, bone, marrow, passion, feeling—
> Because at least the past were passed away—
>   And for the future—(but I write this reeling,
> Having got drunk exceedingly today,
>   So that I seem to stand upon the ceiling)
> I say—the future is a serious matter—
> And so—for God's sake—hock and soda-water!

KAREN WILLIS

Biography of Lord Byron

DOMINUS DE BYRON

The ten-year-old boy had known since age six that he would inherit a title at some point in the future; still, he could hardly fathom it when the event occurred. Enrolled at the Aberdeen Grammar School as Geo. Bayron Gordon, the stocky redhead heard his new title with no warning in Latin during roll call on May 22, 1798: "Dominus de Byron—Lord Byron." His curious classmates staring, he stood speechless, then burst into tears.

His later friend, John Cam Hobhouse, records, "Byron himself told me that he was sent for by the master of the school who gave him some cake & wine & and told him that his paternal great uncle was dead and he was now a lord—Byron added that the little treat and the respectful manner of the master gave him at once high notions of his new dignity." (Marchand, 44) The youth had suddenly advanced to the elite status of possessing social rank and fortune in class-conscious Regency England. He had become the sixth Baron Byron of Rochdale, thus Lord Byron, heir to the Byron peerage of Rochdale, and the estates of Newstead in Nottinghamshire. But the next day in Aberdeen, the newest Lord Byron studied himself in the mirror. Then he asked his mother, as the news spread to their middle class neighbors, "whether she perceived any difference in him since he had been made a lord, as he perceived none himself." (Marchand, 44)

Byron's upbringing had not prepared him for the privileges or responsibilities of nobility. As critic John Wain writes, he was "the child of a shabby-genteel mother and a raffish father, nurtured in [a] side street and suddenly flung into the life of an English *milord*." (162) However, the young milord's parents each claimed a proud lineage. On his father's side, the Byrons held lands in North England at the time of William the Conqueror. When Henry VIII ordered all monasteries dissolved, Sir John Byron bought the Priory of Newstede, converting the Gothic church and priory, with its open court and fountain, to his country estate.

Byron's great uncle, William, the fifth Lord Byron, earned his nickname, the Wicked Lord, by stabbing a neighbor during a duel by candlelight in a locked room. He carried loaded pistols and built a small structure known as "Folly Castle" near the lake at Newstead, adding two turreted forts where he waged war games with his servants, using scaled down boats. His wife left him, probably because of his relationship with a servant woman. Increasingly poor, reclusive, and eccentric, the old lord let pet crickets crawl over him, whipping them with straws. At his death, the crickets swarmed out of the house.

The Wicked Lord cut all ties with his relatives after his son married a woman of no fortune. When his grandson died in 1794, his grandnephew George Gordon Byron became heir presumptive. The old lord took no interest in preparing the boy for life as a nobleman. Not caring about his heir, the Wicked Lord nearly stripped the land of its ancient oaks, and he slaughtered and sold thousands of deer. Desperate for money, he illegally leased the family coalmines.

Byron's grandfather, the Wicked Lord's brother, was a vice-admiral nicknamed Foul Weather Jack because he never sailed without greeting a storm. He survived a shipwreck, then published a narrative telling how he avoided starvation by eating the paw and skin of his favorite dog. His poet grandson later borrowed the incident for the shipwreck scene in his famous long narrative poem, *Don Juan*.

Byron's father, Captain John Byron, the Admiral's oldest son, fought for the British in the American Revolutionary War. He was dubbed Mad Jack because of his high spending, gambling, and affairs. Offended by his son's irresponsible habits, the Admiral disowned him.

In 1778, Mad Jack had an affair with the married Lady Carmarthon, the mother of three children. Enraged, her husband divorced her, and she wed Mad Jack. They left scandal and English creditors behind by moving to France, where Captain Byron promptly consumed his wife's fortune. She gave birth to their daughter Augusta in 1783 but died on January 26, 1784. Having lost his wife's income, Mad Jack headed back to England to find another heiress. Handsome and polished, he captivated twenty-year-old Catherine Gordon.

Byron's mother, Catherine Gordon of Gight, traced her pedigree back to James I of Scotland. The Gordons were prone to staging raids on their neighbors, but by the seventeenth century, they settled into more civilized lives. The eleventh laird married into the wealthy Duff family. He died leaving Catherine as thirteenth heir to the estate of Gight. Catherine, though wealthy, grew into an unsophisticated, stocky, superstitious, extremely moody young woman. Raised in strict Calvinist religious tradition by her conservative grandmother, she was not prepared for Mad Jack Byron when they met in Bath in 1785.

They married on May 13, 1785, and returned to Scotland. Although her beloved Captain Byron's spending frightened Catherine, she could not deny him anything. By 1787, he had squandered Catherine's fortune except for a portion kept in trust for her. The Gight estate had to be sold.

The Byron Gordons, as they were known, fled England ahead of creditors and settled in Paris. Four-year-old Augusta left Captain Byron's sister's home to live with them. Catherine not only nursed Augusta through a serious illness, but also took her back to London to await the birth of the couple's son. Captain Byron followed, but so did more trouble.

The future poet and sixth Lord Byron came into the world on January 22, 1788, with a deformed right foot, diagnosed as a clubfoot. The heel was drawn up and the sole turned inward. At first doctors thought the foot could be corrected by use of a special shoe. Although various shoes and braces were tried, Byron would limp noticeably all his life.

The Byrons moved often, always just ahead of creditors, with Mad Jack continuing to outspend their income. Finally, in 1789, Catherine left him, taking their son back to Aberdeen, where she could live modestly but respectably thanks to her trust. An attempted reconciliation in the cramped Aberdeen apartments failed.

By 1790, Mad Jack returned to France, where he carried on affairs with actresses and chambermaids. He only made one known written reference to his son in a letter written to his sister in February 1791: "For my son, I am happy to hear he is well, but for his walking, 'tis impossible, as he is club-footed." (Marchand, 31) On August 2, 1791, when Byron was three and a half, his father died. Byron told a later companion, "I was not so young when my father died, but that I perfectly remember him; and had a very early horror of matrimony, from the sight of domestic broils ... He seemed born for his own ruin and that of the other sex." (Marchand, 32)

Catherine had suffered the loss of her fortune and her wayward husband. She devoted the rest of her life to her son, although subjecting him always to her temper and sharp tongue. Byron's deformed foot caused her much concern. He often lost his temper over tactless comments made about it by her or others, such as the fishwives of Aberdeen. These women provokingly called him "Mrs. Byron's crookit deevil." (Drinkwater, 95)

Once, a nurse met the Byrons' maid walking with him and commented, "What a pretty boy Byron is! What a pity he has such a leg!" Byron hit her with a little whip he carried, shouting, "Dinna speak of it!" (Marchand, 33) The foot caused conflict between mother and son. According to biographer John Drinkwater, when they fought she might call him "a lame brat," (99) and he responded by accusing her of some behavior at his birth that caused the defect.

However, Byron did not let his foot keep him from cricket and other games. Although it caused him to become combative, he sometimes joked about it himself. Once, teaming up with another boy who also had a clubfoot, he invited everyone to "Come and see the twa laddies with the twa club feet going up Broad Street." (Marchand, 40)

Byron's childhood was not as miserable as one might think. Following an attack of scarlet fever when he was eight, Byron went to the Scottish highlands with his mother to convalesce. He loved rugged, solitary mountains from then on. He also loved pranks. Once, he dressed his pillow in his clothes and threw it out the window to frighten his mother and aunt below. When the aunt demanded he be punished, he butted her with his head. Occasionally, in St. Paul's Church in Aberdeen, he was observed poking pins into his mother's plump gloved arms during the service.

Byron felt his first romantic attraction at only age eight, when he met a distant cousin, Mary Duff. He obsessed about her dark hair and hazel eyes. As an adult he wrote in his diary, "I have been thinking lately a good deal of Mary Duff. How very odd that I should have been so utterly, devotedly fond of that girl, at an age when I could neither feel passion, nor know the meaning of the word." (Marchand, 41)

Implications are that another experience involved sexual molestation rather than idealized love. May Gray, the family maid, introduced Byron to the beauty of the Psalms, even as she preached the doctrine that some people are predestined to evil. But May Gray also beat Byron, drank to excess, and was promiscuous. She contributed to his future contempt for pious hypocrites and affected his relationships with women. When Byron was only nine, she "used to come to bed to him and play tricks with his person." (Wain, 158)

Byron would write, "My passions were developed very early—so early, that few would believe me, if I were to state the period, and the facts which accompanied it." (Wain, 158) Catherine dismissed the maid after John Hanson, who became the family lawyer and business advisor, reported some of what the young Lord Byron finally confided in him.

Byron's academic education was uneven. At five, he attended school in a noisy, grimy room with bad lighting and holes in the floor, run by Mr. John Bowers. When Catherine discovered he could not read, she briefly hired tutors. She enrolled him at age seven in the Aberdeen Grammar School, where the students only studied Latin. After the morning spent there, he crossed a churchyard for an hour of Mr. Dunbar's writing school.

Byron devoured books even while at grammar school. Travels and histories came first, and he loved *The Arabian Nights*. Knolle's *Turkish History* influenced his later attraction to the Eastern Mediterranean islands and countries as well as the Asian aspects in his poetry. He read novels, eventually thousands of them. He identified with the fatherless hero of the novel *Zeluco*, spoiled by an indulgent mother and destined by forces beyond his control to commit bad acts. At first he hated poetry, but he admired the Old Testament, especially the story of Cain and Abel.

Byron's early political influences were mixed. He was born one year before the beginning of the French Revolution, with which his mother Catherine sympathized. He grew up and attended school with the rough-and-tumble lower middle class Scottish people of his Aberdeen neighborhood, which also contributed to his liberal views. Still, Byron was a snob about his title, even though he barely knew what to do with it at first. Critic John Wain writes, "A childhood spent in genteel poverty, suddenly cut across by the entirely unexpected reversion of the title, had left him with a basic uncertainty as to which world he really belonged in." (166) According to biographer John Drinkwater, snobbery became "one of his least amiable characteristics. Byron, in his later years, might sometimes forget that he was a gentleman, but he would never forget that he was a lord." (98)

After Catherine sold the family furniture in August 1798, they traveled to Newstead. Arriving at the tollgate just inside Sherwood Forest, Catherine feigned ignorance and asked to whom the mansion at Newstead belonged. The toll-keeper said it had been Lord Byron's, but he was now dead. When Catherine asked who the next heir was, the toll-keeper replied, "[T]hey say it is a little boy who lives at Aberdeen." (Maurois, 34) They drove past stumps of oaks, pinewoods, and dilapidated farms until they came in sight of the ruined abbey on the edge of a wide lake, great and peaceful. John Hanson and his wife waited there to greet them.

Both Byron and Catherine fell in love with Newstead, but Hanson discouraged them from moving in because of the abbey's condition. The back of the great building had lost its roof, and hay filled the reception hall and parlor, which had recently served as stables. Every wall, floor, and ceiling needed repair.

Young Byron thrilled to hear the old servant Joe Murray, tell stories of the Wicked Lord, and to the news that the ghost of a black-hooded monk haunted the Abbey. Byron began improvements by planting an acorn with the idea that as the oak grew, so would his fortunes. He also proudly viewed the family coat of arms: a mermaid and chestnut horses surmounting the motto "Crede Byron"—"Trust Byron."

Catherine remained at Newstead to oversee the start of what improvements they could afford, settling Byron with a family in Nottingham. Even at age eleven, Byron took some control of his future. When his mother balked at the expense of a tutor, he wrote to her. He wanted her to hire a Mr. Rogers, saying "—if some plan of this kind is not adopted, I shall be called, or rather branded with the name of a dunce, which you know I could never bear." (Marchand, 51–52)

Catherine hired the tutor, but she also employed a quack doctor named Lavender, who treated Byron's foot by rubbing it with oil, then screwing it into a wooden machine. Rogers expressed his discomfort at tutoring Byron for hours while he had to be in pain from the foot contraption. The young lord bravely replied, "Never mind, Mr. Rogers, you shall not see any sign of it in me." (Marchand, 52) Lavender scandalized Nottingham by sending the new lord limping through the streets to bring the doctor his pint of beer under the threat of a beating. Byron had his revenge on the pompous hypocrite by writing letters at random on a sheet of paper, then asking the doctor what language it was. When Lavender proclaimed it Italian, Byron roared with laughter. It was an early poke at hypocrisy. His later satiric poetry, according to critic John Wain, became "the biggest one-man debunking spree the world has ever seen." (165)

But Byron also experienced deeply serious emotions. On holiday in 1801, he met another cousin, thirteen-year-old Margaret Parker. He would write, "She looked as if she had been made out of a rainbow—all beauty and peace." (Maurois, 42) He wrote his earliest poetry for her. Also during his holidays, his mother consulted a notorious fortune-teller, Mrs. Williams, who announced Byron would marry twice, the second time to a foreigner. She also predicted Byron would experience two dangerous periods. One would be his twenty-seventh year, and the other his thirty-seventh. Byron, who believed in omens, never forgot her words.

Catherine asked the courts for more money from her underage son's estate. As a result, she was granted a Civil List Pension and could move to London to find better opportunities for Byron's education and medical treatment.

John Hanson found a school for Byron, Dr. Glennie's Academy at Dulwich. He also persuaded Byron's cousin, Lord Carlisle, to become the boy's guardian, although Hanson would remain manager of Byron's finances. Carlisle was elegant, politically powerful, and refined. He and the noisy, awkward, badly-dressed Catherine could not stand each other. Lord Carlisle withdrew from contact with his charge and his charge's mother.

Catherine kept Byron home from school for periods of time and embarrassed him by showing up periodically for loud arguments with Dr. Glennie. One of Byron's schoolmates, hearing Catherine's haranguing the schoolmaster said, "Byron, your mother is a fool." Byron answered sadly, "I know it." (Maurois, 41)

But the adults in his life now made a decision that would help Byron learn to be a sophisticated nobleman with a first-rate education. At age thirteen and a half, Byron entered Harrow, one of the great public schools of England.

HARROW AND HEARTACHES

When Byron went "to school at Harrow and then on to Cambridge," according to scholar Gilbert Highet, "he was thrown into a rough but cheerful society, in which a man needed both wits and guts to make his mark. Byron made his mark." (147)

Hanson introduced him to Dr. Joseph Drury, headmaster at Harrow. Drury faced a handsome adolescent who appeared haughty, reserved, and touchy. The perceptive headmaster would record later that he invited Byron to his study to engage him

> by inquiries as to his former amusements, employments, and associates, but with little or no effect;—and I soon found that a wild mountain colt had been submitted to my management. But there was mind in his eye.... His manner and temper soon convinced me, that he might be led by a silken string to a point, rather than by a cable;—on that principle I acted. (Marchand, 64)

The insightful Drury realized that Byron could not be placed with his own age group at once. He assigned his own son, Henry Drury, to tutor Byron privately until he reached the level with the other boys in his age group. Byron would later write in one of his notes to the Fourth Canto of his long poem *Childe Harold's Pilgrimage*, "The Rev. Dr. Joseph Drury was the best and worthiest friend I ever possessed." (McGann, ed., 204)

Despite Drury's tactful approach, Byron hated Harrow at first. The boys were cruel about his foot; more than once he woke to find his leg in a tub of water. He defended himself with his fists, as he had done in Aberdeen. Byron also felt insecure and awed in the presence of the self-assured older boys of his own rank. To compensate, he made his first friends of boys who were younger and of more humble origins. Biographer John Drinkwater calls such social activity "a not uncommon form of snobbery." (102)

Whatever motivated Byron, he proved the protector of these smaller, younger friends and formed passionate, fiercely jealous friendships with such boys then and later at Cambridge. Whether they were fully experienced homosexual relationships has never been established, although some scholars believe they were.

Noble rank always held Byron's attention. According to author Ian Jack, "[O]n one occasion, when another boy pinched his ear, he threw something at him shouting 'that would teach a fool of an earl to pinch another noble's ear.'" (50) Another time Byron asked a monitor at the school not to be strict with the offenses of a boy who was in trouble. To the question "Why not?" he is said to have replied, "Why, I don't know—except that he is a brother peer.'" (Drinkwater, 103)

The proud young lord could be careless and lazy, so cramming sessions were not unusual. Byron also often forgot or refused to wear the brace a new doctor had prescribed for his foot, especially if it interfered with his taking part in sports with the other boys. From the first he wanted not just to fit in, but to lead. Harrow gradually began to improve for Byron as he forged his own path. However, even though he grew sociable and joined in sports and practical jokes, he also showed a reflective, sometimes melancholy side. One reason for sadness came with news of the death of his beloved cousin, Margaret Parker.

By the time Byron turned fifteen, he had begun to express his depressed as well as humorous moods in poems. He often limped alone to the Harrow churchyard. His favorite spot for contemplation, reading, or writing was the flat blue limestone tomb of one John Peachey, under an old elm, with a view overlooking valleys and forested hills.

Bored by Greek studies and rebellious toward authority figures, Byron clashed with Henry Drury, the headmaster's son. On May 1, 1803, he wrote to his mother,

> To-day in church I was talking to a Boy who was sitting next me; that perhaps was not right, but hear what followed.

After church he spoke not a word to me, but he took this Boy to his pupilroom, where he abused me in a most violent manner, called me blackguard, said he would and could have me expelled from the School and bade me thank his Charity that prevented him ... Is this fit usage for anybody? ... If he had had it in his power to have me expelled, he would long ago have done it ... If I am treated in this manner, I will not stay at this School ... Remember I told you ... If you do not take notice of this, I will leave the School myself... (Drinkwater, 103)

The headmaster apologized for his son. Dr. Drury recognized that Byron possessed a passionate, brilliant mind. When Byron's guardian, Lord Carlisle, inquired as to Byron's progress, Drury answered him with the words, "He has talents, my lord, which *will add lustre to his rank.*" (Marchand, 73)

In the summer of 1803, Byron joined his mother at Burgage Manor, a house she rented near Newstead. The Newstead mansion and park had been leased to Lord Grey de Ruthyn. Lord Grey invited Byron to visit Newstead, and, bored with life at his mother's house, he accepted.

His favorite ride became the three or four miles west down the Bridal Path from Newstead to Annesley Hall. Mary Ann Chaworth, great-niece of the man stabbed by the Wicked Lord, lived there. The lovely eighteen-year-old Mary Ann found fifteen-year-old Byron entertaining. Byron rode to Annesley every morning until the Chaworths invited him to stay over at night. He happily agreed, claiming to have met a ghost in the dark on a late ride back to Newstead.

Byron called Mary Ann the "Morning Star of Annesley." The slightest touch of their hands would excite him. Years later he recalled,

I had to cross in a boat (in which two people only could lie down) a stream which flows under a rock, with the rock so close upon the water as to admit the boat only to be pushed on by a ferryman ... who wades at the stern, stooping all the time. The companion of my transit was M.A.C., with whom I had been long in love, and never told it, though *she* discovered it without. I recollect my sensations but cannot describe them, and it is as well. (Maurois, 53)

Byron treasured a portrait and ring Mary Ann gave him. His heart belonged to her completely. Unfortunately, her heart belonged to Mr. John Musters, a country gentleman whose focus was mainly riding to the hounds. In her indifference she inflicted a humiliation Byron would never forget. One night as he stood at the bottom of the stairs at Annesley, he overheard Mary Ann say to her maid, "Do you think I could care anything for that lame boy?" (Maurois, 54) Byron rushed into the night and ran all the way to Newstead. But, hopelessly in love, he went back the next morning. Much to his mother's distress, he also refused to return to Harrow.

Besides his desperate, unrequited love, some mysterious break took place with Lord Grey. Although Byron never revealed exactly what happened, he hinted that unwanted sexual advances from Lord Grey caused their rift. A disillusioned Byron finally returned to Harrow in January 1804, just after he turned sixteen.

The next woman of interest to enter Byron's life was his half-sister Augusta. Reared by her mother's relatives, she wanted to know her little brother. They began to exchange letters. Catherine had begun a romance with Lord Grey, so Byron became more and more estranged from her and welcomed his sister as a sympathetic friend and confidante.

Around this time he also gained a true friend in Elizabeth Pigot, a few years older and part of a family who lived across the green from his mother at Southwell. They met at a party, and her first impression was of

a fat bashful boy, with his hair combed straight over his forehead ... The next morning Mrs. Byron brought him to call ... I mentioned that I had seen the character Gabriel Lackbrain very well performed. His mother getting up ... [and he] making a formal bow, I, in allusion to the play, said 'Good by, Gaby.' His countenance lighted up, his handsome mouth displayed a broad grin, all his shyness vanished, never to return. (Marchand, 82–83)

Back at Harrow, life improved a great deal. Byron did well at oratory, making speeches that encouraged his ambitions for a career in politics. Older now and with a better knowledge of the world, he made friends more easily and indulged in his early passion for books. By his own account, he "read eating, read in bed, read when no one else reads ...." (Marchand, 84)

Unfortunately, Byron's difficulties with authority existed as strongly as his ease in reading. Even the understanding Dr. Drury finally suggested Byron not return to Harrow after the Christmas holidays because his conduct had given the headmaster "much trouble and uneasiness." (Marchand, 92) Not wanting to appear expelled, Byron negotiated a return.

Home in Southwell that summer, Byron enjoyed spending time with the Pigot family and joined in community theatricals. But disputes with his mother intensified. He wrote to Augusta, "In former days she spoilt me; now she is altered to the contrary...." (Marchand, 86–87) Augusta arranged for his renewed contacts with Lord Carlisle. Pleased by Byron's conflicts with Catherine, Lord Carlisle finally showed a bit more interest in his ward.

During his last year at Harrow, Byron blossomed, finding greater popularity among the other students. He participated in all sports, especially swimming, where his foot caused no problems. He also started a lifelong practice of carving his name in wood or stone to mark where he had been. Andre Maurois writes, "The holy of holies at Harrow was an old class-room, the Fourth Form Room, its walls lined with dark oak panelling a full three centuries old. As a monitor, Byron had become one of the guardians of this sanctuary, and three times he had carved a bold vigorous BYRON in the wood, amid many illustrious names." (70)

Besides his fierce, impassioned friendships with boys such as the beautiful Lord Delawarr, Byron's peace was marred only by Dr. Drury's retirement. The question of who would succeed that beloved headmaster became a political disaster. Two candidates, the doctor's brother, Mark Drury, and a mathematics teacher, Rev. George Butler, headed the list. Tom Wildman led the pro-Drury students until another gentleman told him, "Byron, I know, won't join, because he doesn't choose to act second to anyone; but by giving up the leadership to him, you may at once secure him." (Maurois, 72) Wildman agreed, and Byron took over. In the end, the Governors' votes tied, and the Archbishop of Canterbury made the final choice: Dr. Butler.

A revolt soon followed after the appointment of Dr. Butler. Byron carried loaded pistols; some boys wanted to sprinkle gunpowder on the path Dr. Butler took to the Fourth Form Room to eradicate him. Because the precious names carved by their forefathers in the paneling would also be destroyed, they gave up that plan. But in a frustrated rage, Byron ripped the iron gratings from Butler's house, later using the excuse that "they darkened the hall." (Maurois, 73)

Byron wrote and circulated satires featuring Butler renamed as Pomposus. As a senior, Byron received a customary invitation to dine with Headmaster Butler at the term's end. Byron did the unheard of, and refused. Not until years later, during a visit to Harrow, did Byron amend his differences with Butler; the two ended as friends.

Throughout that last bittersweet year at Harrow, Byron and Augusta's friendship deepened through letters. He invited her to hear him give a speech, he complained about his mother, and with a newfound cynicism, he teased his engaged sister about love. When Catherine railed at Augusta for furthering Byron's contacts with Lord Carlisle, Byron wrote, "Believe me, dearest Augusta, not ten thousand *such* mothers, or indeed any mothers, could induce me to give you up." (Drinkwater, 116)

Byron cherished this easy closeness to his half-sister. He still felt shy around strangers, mortified about his foot, embarrassed by his uncouth mother, and stung to the heart by Mary Ann Chaworth. With the exception of his pal Elizabeth Pigot, he appeared painfully awkward around women. Andre Maurois writes, "When presented to a woman, he was so deeply troubled that he could do nothing but count under his breath: 'One, two, three, four, five, six, seven.... One, two, three, four, five, six, seven....' He adored them, and hated them. He hated them because he adored them." (60)

Byron felt most at ease at Harrow. With wits and courage he had made his mark. He even joined in partying at Mother Barnard's, the local inn, where he once roared, "This bottle's the sun of our table!" (Marchand, 96) He dreaded leaving the now comfortable world of the school. "I so much disliked leaving Harrow," he included in his book, *Detached Thoughts*, "that though it was time (I being seventeen), it broke my very rest for the last quarter with counting the days that remained." (Marchand, 96)

He had a sharp sense of time's quick passage. He wrote on the flyleaf of his *Scriptores Graeci*, "George Gordon Byron, Wednesday, June 26 A.D. 1805, 3 quarters of an hour past 3 o'clock in the afternoon, 3d school,—Calvert, monitor, Tom Wildman on my left hand, and Long on my right. Harrow on the Hill." (Marchand, 96)

Adding to life at Harrow, Byron's foot improved at last so that he only needed a regular boot over a corrective shoe. He ended his school days by playing in the final cricket match of the year against archrival Eton on August 2, 1805. It was a triumph, even if a qualified one. Henry Long, brother to Byron's friend Edward Noel Long, wrote, "The most curious thing was, that Lord Byron, though lame, was one of the eleven: he was always ambitious of doing as other boys but in this instance, was obliged to have somebody run for him." (Marchand, 98)

Byron took great pride in his part in the game even though Eton beat Harrow. That night, the teams shared a friendly dinner, got drunk, and moved on to the Haymarket Theatre, where they "kicked up a row." (Marchand, 99) The next day he returned to Southwell. Still in love with Mary Chaworth, he learned of her marriage in a cruel way. An eyewitness, probably Elizabeth Pigot, told biographer Moore, "His mother said, 'Byron, I have some news for you.'—'Well, what is it?—' 'Take out your handkerchief first, for you will want it.' —'Nonsense!'—'Take out your handkerchief, I say.' He did so, to humour her. 'Miss Chaworth is married.' An expression, very peculiar, impossible to describe, passed over his pale face, and he hurried his handkerchief into his pocket, saying, with an affected air of coldness and nonchalance, 'Is that all?'—'Why, I expected you would have been plunged in grief!'—He made no reply, and soon began to talk about something else." (Marchand, 99–100)

It is not surprising that even though he was not due to start his studies at Cambridge until October 24, Byron escaped Southwell for London on September 23, 1805. As Augusta observed, the Harrow years had seen a change in her young brother.

FRIENDS, DEBTS, AND PUBLISHED POEMS

Byron described himself in October 1805 as "miserable and untoward to a degree. I was wretched at leaving Harrow—wretched at going to

Cambridge instead of Oxford ... wretched from some private domestic circumstances of different kinds, and consequently about as unsocial as a wolf taken from the troop." (Marchand, 101)

However, Cambridge meant independence. The Court of Chancery permitted him 500 pounds annually from his estate revenues. He had rooms of his own, a gray horse named Oateater, and a manservant. He soon felt "as a German Prince who coins his own cash, or a Cherokee Chief who coins no cash at all, but enjoys what is more precious, Liberty. I speak in raptures of that Goddess because my amiable Mama was so despotic ...." (Marchand, 77)

Cambridge men of rank and privilege considered drinking and gambling fashionable, but reading a bore. They argued and punned endlessly. Even though he loved to read and disliked heavy drinking, Byron wrote to Hanson ordering a dozen each of port, sherry, claret, and Madeira. He wrote to his lawyer's son that "College improves in everything but Learning. Nobody here seems to look into an Author, ancient or modern, if they can avoid it." (Marchand, 102)

Wearing gold-embroidered gowns and hats instead of normal academic caps, noblemen at Harrow held themselves aloof. But Byron still spent time with untitled people like his friend from Harrow, Edward Long. He often listened to Long play the flute or violoncello in the evening. By day they dove into the river Cam's fourteen-foot depth after plates, shillings, or eggs, and read, or went riding. Byron began composing poetry again.

Aristocratic frivolity bored him, but he did not completely give up late-night parties. He spent money lavishly and by the end of November was writing to Hanson complaining that funds he expected had not arrived. Hanson horrified Byron by responding that Catherine might visit her son to personally reproach him for overspending. Byron was now in dire financial straits. During his Christmas vacation in London, he asked Augusta to be joint security on a loan from moneylenders. Knowing the high interest this would involve, she declined, causing a coldness between them. His landlady in London did sign.

At this time Byron had formed a romantic friendship with a choirboy, John Edleston, at Trinity Chapel, and he suffered over their separation. He described their love as pure, so again, though he felt intense devotion to the boy, the love may not have been consummated.

As a diversion Byron took up fencing. Through his fencing master, Byron met Gentleman Jackson, a famous boxer. Byron spent time with them and others in the theatrical and sporting worlds. When his loan finally came through, he wrote to Catherine, "Improvement at an English University to a Man of Rank is, you know, impossible, and the very Idea is *ridiculous*." (Marchand, 110) Instead of his return to Cambridge he proposed an extended trip abroad.

Waiting for her and his guardian's responses, he lived the life of a playboy. Catherine, fearing that she had a second Mad Jack on her hands, wrote in desperation to Hanson: "That Boy will be the death of me & drive me mad—I much fear he is already ruined; at eighteen!!!" (Marchand, 111)

Byron asked Hanson for more money, then returned to Cambridge. Extravagance followed extravagance: a carriage, horses, servants in livery, a silver hunting watch, gold chains, gold seal, a key and an engraving. As a young dandy, he would even bring his mistress and fencing and boxing instructors up from London. But he also wrote poems in Cambridge, in London, and back at his mother's home in Southwell, where he had to go since he was out of money. That necessity was unfortunate. The Pigot family witnessed one scene between mother and son that involved Catherine hurling the fireplace shovel and tongs at Byron's head.

But in calmer moments, Byron worked seriously on poetry, writing at night and walking to the Pigot's house to show his work to Elizabeth. She offered to copy it for publication.

Byron worked to prepare a volume of poems for the printer, John Ridge. Aside from poetry and the Pigot family, he felt nothing but discontent at Southwell. He wrote to Hanson, "Wine and women have dished your humble servant, not a soul to be had ... I am condemned to exist (I cannot say live) at this center of dullness till my lease of infancy expires." (Untermeyer, 385)

Before arriving in Southwell, the 5' 8" Byron weighed 202 pounds. He wrote to Hanson describing a system of exercise and fasting. He ran daily wearing seven waistcoats and a great coat, took hot baths, and was eating "only a quarter of a pound of Butcher's Meat in 24 hours, no Suppers or Breakfast, only one Meal a Day; drink no Malt liquor, but a little Wine, and take Physic occasionally ... & my Clothes have been taken in nearly *half a yard*." (Marchand, 128)

He participated in theatricals and flirtations but according to Marchand, Byron gave romance only "cynical attention. Since his frustrated passion for Mary Chaworth he felt the capacity for attachments had been burned out of him." (Marchand, 117)

Byron's first book of poetry, *Fugitive Pieces*, appeared anonymously in November 1806. He gave a copy to Reverend John Thomas Beder, who objected to the erotic nature of the poem, "To Mary," probably written about Byron's Southwell mistress. Such frank poetry outraged the gossips of Southwell. Upset, Byron recalled every copy he had distributed and burned them. In January 1807, he produced a revised volume, entitled *Poems on Various Occasions*, calling it "*vastly* correct and miraculously chaste." (Jack, 50)

His second book of poems, *Hours of Idleness*, published in March 1807, carried his name on the title page as George Gordon, Lord Byron, A Minor. Some of the poems had been written at Harrow, some later. Most suffered from immaturity and imitation.

Through his efforts, in 1807 Byron reappeared at Cambridge triumphantly lean and published. His friends now included John Cam Hobhouse, who would be a later traveling companion. Hobhouse introduced Byron to fun-loving Charles Skinner Matthews who occupied Byron's rooms during his time at Southwell. Matthews advised visitors to take care even in touching the door because the tutor had advised him when he moved in "not to damage any of the moveables, for Lord Byron, Sir, is a young man of *tumultuous passions*." (Marchand, 131)

Byron also renewed his passionate friendship with Edleston, imagining that they might live together after he attained his majority and could afford to provide for his protégé. Irked by rules against his bulldog, Smut, being at Cambridge, and maintaining that no rules applied to bears, he bought a tame bear, lodging it in the tower above his rooms. Byron enjoyed creating a sensation by taking the bear for walks, and he joked about having it sit for a fellowship. After it frightened another student, Byron regretfully shipped it back to Newstead.

Byron also began a novel, as well as a long satire on the poetry of the day, which Ridge refused to publish for fear of libel suits. Meanwhile, the poet made more friends, including Scrope Davies, who taught him how to gamble. He joined the liberal Cambridge Whig Club, too. The classical scholar Francis Hodgson tried unsuccessfully to convert Byron to orthodox religious beliefs. Byron may not have agreed with him, but their's and his other Cambridge friendships lasted until death.

At Christmas in 1807, Byron moved to Dorant's Hotel in London to assist in distribution of *Hours of Idleness*. There, he continued to dream of a European tour once he reached age twenty-one and adulthood. Meanwhile, in London until July 1808, he fell into further debt, promiscuity, and late nights. He settled a sixteen-year-old girl named Caroline in Brompton. She dressed in men's clothing and passed as his younger brother. Eventually he rented a little house at Brighton, where he took her boating on Sundays. Wherever they went, Byron arranged for them to sleep in separate beds, a practice he continued with his future mistresses. The relationship was not exclusive on Byron's part.

Byron raged over bad reviews of *Hours of Idleness*. One even suggested he should have been whipped at Harrow except the masters must have had "undue respect for lords' bottoms." That caused Byron to issue a challenge for a duel, although nothing came of it. The harshest review of *Hours of Idleness* appeared on February 11, 1808, in the *Edinburgh Review*, in part saying, "[Byron's] effusions are spread over a dead flat, and can no more get above or below the level than if they were so much stagnant water...." (Drinkwater, 124)

Byron took his revenge in the medium for which he was attacked. He returned to work on his satire, "British Bards," adding and revising what would eventually become the searing *English Bards and Scotch Reviewers*. He worried, too, about obtaining his degree. According to Cambridge rules, he had to attend nine terms to earn his degree, but he had only attended three full terms and parts of two others. Cambridge's leniency toward nobles worked in his favor when he received his M.A. degree in July 1808.

In spite of that success, poor health from his debauched life in London and his reaction to bad reviews of *Hours of Idleness* sank Byron into depression. He recovered by vacationing in Brighton with Caroline, his boxing friend Jackson, and Hobhouse.

In September, Byron returned to Newstead to oversee badly needed repairs. He found his oak nearly choked by grass and tended it gently back to health. He fixed a room for himself with a window overlooking swans on the lake, the Wicked Lord's forts, and more distant hills. His room also had a built-in staircase that descended to a study and drawing room. A second door opened onto an empty apartment that the servants claimed the black-hooded monk occupied. Byron furnished a few other rooms for guests, but most of the abbey remained empty ruins.

He often rode over the grounds or wrote in the garden, using one of the oaks cut down by the Wicked Lord as a desk. He accepted one invitation to dine with his old love Mary Ann Chaworth and her husband. Byron's most painful moment came when their two-year-old daughter, clearly a blend of both parents, was brought in. After that he avoided socializing with neighbors. He preferred the company of his visiting Cambridge friends and his Newfoundland, Boatswain. His heart broke when Boatswain caught rabies. After nursing the dog by hand until the end, Byron insisted a vault be raised for him on the site of the old monks' chapel.

Alone by November, Byron revised the satire *English Bards and Scotch Reviewers*. Legal entanglements over his property at Rochdale and accumulated debt led to his writing to Hanson, "I suppose it will end in my marrying a *Golden Dolly* or blowing my brains out; it does not much matter which, the remedies are nearly alike." (Marchand, 163)

When his gardener unearthed the skull of one of the long dead monks, Byron had it polished and set in silver on four balls, to be used as a drinking cup. He wrote, in "Lines Inscribed upon a Cup Formed from a Skull,"

> Start not—nor deem my spirit fled:
> In me behold the only skull,
> From which, unlike a living head,
> Whatever flows is never dull.
> (Marchand, 164)

In a pensive mood, Byron returned to London to spend his twenty-first birthday in solitude. There, he grieved on learning Edward Long had drowned. Byron added to his old inscription in the *Scriptores Graeci* of Harrow days, "B. January 9, 1809.—Of the four persons whose names are here mentioned, one is dead, another in a distant climate, *all* separated, and not five years have elapsed since they sat together in school, and none are yet twenty-one years of age." (Maurois, 115)

He asked Hanson to represent him at Newstead on his birthday and organize a celebration with an ox roast and a ball for his tenants. Byron also instructed his lawyer to set up annuities for child support for a servant girl who was carrying his child.

Byron kept busy in London putting final touches on *English Bards and Scotch Reviewers*. He had always admired the ideals of the French Revolution and wrote as a rebellious critic of England's conservative imperialism. Scholar Jerome J. McGann says that in his satire Byron "singles out a few *individuals* for praise and honour, but his attack is launched at the culture as a whole, where he is able to see no party, no class, no institution with which to identify. English culture is represented in a state of crisis, and Byron is but a voice crying in its wilderness." (McGann, xiv–xv)

Byron asked a friend, Robert Charles Dallas, to read the satire and help find a publisher. This proved challenging, as Byron spared no one—not critics, popular English poets, or even his aloof guardian, Lord Carlisle. Byron had reason for anger at Lord Carlisle. Although it was customary for a relative or friend to introduce a new member into the House of Lords, Lord Carlisle gave only procedural advice. As a result, Byron had to prove his legitimacy by producing family birth and other records. Byron whiled away the time by reading political memoirs and histories to prepare for politics.

On the morning of March 13, 1809, eight months after Byron had left Cambridge, Dallas dropped in to find Byron alone and embarrassed. Byron asked Dallas to go with him to Parliament. Dallas related that while they waited in an antechamber for an officer to inform the Lord Chancellor of Byron's arrival, Byron grew more pale, nervous, and indignant. When Byron took his oath, the Chancellor walked to him, smiled, and extended a hand in welcome. Byron only "made a stiff bow, and put the tips of his fingers into a hand, the amiable offer of which demanded the whole of his." (Marchand, 170) The Chancellor returned to his seat. Byron later explained that he did not want to give the Chancellor the wrong impression. Byron would join neither the conservative Tories nor liberal Whigs. Instead, he would go abroad.

Byron's estate revenues would have made him rich once he reached age twenty-one, but his staggering debts had to be paid. However, this did not slow his spending. He visited Catherine, then went to Newstead for a bit of revelry before realizing his goal of travel.

He invited several friends to join him; they dressed in monks' costumes, enjoyed Byron's wine cellar, drank from the skull cup, and played jokes. While the young men entertained themselves with the servant girls, they also found time to write, as Byron always would, in England or abroad. And he was about to realize that dream of travel to distant lands, a journey that would provide adventure and material for the beginning of his life's work.

TRAVEL AND SUCCESS

As they left England, Byron and Hobhouse's entourage included three servants from Newstead. Byron took longtime servant Joe Murray and young page Robert Rushton as far as Gibraltar, believing sea air would improve the old man's health. William Fletcher would accompany Byron much farther.

Sentimental, Byron had miniatures painted of Harrow friends and obsessed for weeks after Delawarr declined a last visit, having promised to take female relatives shopping. But, nostalgic moments aside, Byron wrote to Catherine at Newstead, "I leave England without regret, and without a wish to revisit anything it contains, except yourself, and your present residence." (Maurois, 125)

Byron's party finally sailed from Falmouth bound for Lisbon on June 26, 1809. They found a dirty city showing signs of recent battles, as Europe still suffered through the Napoleonic wars, with England and France committed enemies. However, Byron and Hobhouse reacted with the most shock to witnessing the sometimes brutal power of the Catholic Church over its people.

Byron proved most adaptable to foreign life. He rode often through the beautiful scenery, swam in the Tagus River, and enjoyed observing native Portuguese. Good-naturedly putting up with mosquito bites and diarrhea, he wrote, "Comfort must not be expected by folks that go apleasuring." (Maurois, 125) After two weeks, Byron and Hobhouse rode horseback to Seville and Cadiz. They wore English regimental style uniforms for safety in Spain and Portugal. Both countries hated the French and respected the English. The travelers rose at 4:00 a.m., covered about seventy miles a day, and slept in primitive inns.

In Seville they engaged in sightseeing and stayed at the home of two unmarried sisters. One invited Byron to share her bed, a proposition he declined. But the passionate personality of the Spanish attracted Byron. He felt both captivated and repelled by the romance and brutality when he witnessed his first bullfight. He always sought out English society in foreign places, but he also visited with both common and noble Spaniards. A meeting with Admiral Cordova's daughter at the opera left Byron charmed. He expressed his admiration poetically in "The Girl of Cadiz."

The flirtation was short-lived because Byron sailed as planned for Gibraltar. There, each evening, Byron and Hobhouse climbed its famous rock to view Africa as the sun set. From Gibraltar they moved on to Sardinia where Byron showed both his moody and pompous sides on the trip. By day he could be playful, pistol shooting with other passengers, but at night he took a place alone at the mizzen shrouds, gazing at the moon and sea. He also kept to a vegetarian diet, as his tendency to gain weight followed wherever he went.

From Sardinia, they continued to Malta, where Byron, ever mindful of his noble rank, held off from disembarking because he expected a salute from the battery. According to fellow passenger John Galt, "[T]he guns were sulky, and evinced no respect of persons; so that late in the afternoon ... the two magnates were obliged to come on shore, and slip into the city unnoticed and unknown." (Marchand, 197)

The British governor helped them find a suitable residence. Byron entered society in Malta. He took morning lessons in Arabic, bathed in the afternoon, dined with friends, then attended the theater. In the course of all this, he fell in love with Mrs. Constance Spencer Smith, a woman who had once fled for her life from Napoleon. Byron planned to go on to Constantinople, and Mrs. Spencer Smith to Cadiz, but they arranged to meet in one year. Before they parted, Byron nearly fought a duel to defend her honor, but the officer who had been offensive apologized.

Byron's most colorful adventures began when he left Malta on a brig of war and arrived in Turkey eight days later. He traveled into Albania to Prevesa, then to Jannina and inland to Tepelene to be a guest of Ali Pasha at his country palace. Byron adored the wild Albanian countryside and its peoples' rich crimson and gold costumes. The powerful Ottoman ruler showed true Arabic hospitality. Writing to Catherine about his first meeting with the pasha, Byron wrote, "He said he was certain I was a man of birth because I had small ears, curling hair, & little white hands ... He told me to consider him as a father ... & said he looked on me as a son." (McGann, 972)

For Byron, Ali Pasha resembled his fictional hero, Zeluco, come to life. Hospitality to friends matched the pasha's cruelty to enemies, which included roasting them alive. Biographer Maurois writes, "Love of power, scorn of moral and social laws, a taste for enwrapping mystery—the whole personality of Ali moved Byron profoundly." (Maurois, 130)

When Byron and Hobhouse left, the pasha provided them with a guard of fifty Albanian soldiers. Flanked by these fierce warriors, they revisited Jannina, this time traveling further east to see sites of ancient Greek ruins. Byron felt inspired to record his own thoughts during this adventure and began a long narrative poem, *Childe Harold's Pilgrimage*.

They sailed next for Patras on a galiot provided by the pasha. Unfortunately, the Turks made better soldiers than sailors. All on board nearly drowned in a shipwreck. Byron wrote to Catherine,

> ... Fletcher yelled after his wife, the Greeks called on all the Saints, the Musselmen on Alla, the Captain burst into tears & ran below deck telling us to call on God—I did what I could to console Fletcher but finding him incorrigible wrapped myself up in my Albanian capote (an immense cloak) & lay down on deck.... (McGann, 973–974)

The Greek sailors on board steered them into a bay, where an Albanian chief gave them food and lodging and an evening of folk dance around the fire. Byron and company then moved on to Missolonghi in Greece. Greek scenery and ruins inspired Byron, who had admired the ancient land since childhood. At Delphi, Byron and Hobhouse carved their names into temple columns, a schoolboy's act they would repeat on a visit to Attica.

The Greeks' enslavement under the Turks enraged Byron. He wanted a people with such a glowing heritage of courage and freedom to revolt. His sympathies with the Greek people extended to a sharp critical view of Lord Elgin, the Englishman who appropriated many of the country's marble masterpieces and shipped them to England.

Even as he bemoaned the Greeks' bondage, Byron fell in love again. His Greek landlady had three beautiful daughters, Teresa, Marianna, and Katinka. Infatuated with dark-eyed Teresa, he wrote his poem "The Maid of Athens." As contentedly as they lived in Greece, when the opportunity arose to take passage on the English sloop-of-war the *Pylades* on March 5, 1810, the two pilgrims accepted at once. Docking at Smyrna, Byron continued *Childe Harold*, but disappointed by Hobhouse's reaction, he packed the manuscript away in his luggage.

From Smyrna they traveled around Lesbos and saw the Dardanelles, the narrow passage that separates Europe from Asia. The Hellespont, a tide flowing between two high banks of the Dardonelles, is the setting of the classic story of Hero and Leander. While his ship lay at anchor near the plains of Troy, Byron decided to swim the Hellespont.

On his third try, along with one Lieutenant Ekenhead, Byron succeeded. He proudly added to Hobhouse's diary entry describing the event: "The total distance E & myself swam was more than 4 miles the current very strong and cold, some large fish near us when half across, we were not fatigued but a little chilled; did it with little difficulty." (Marchand, 238) The feat took Byron one hour and ten minutes. In letters to friends in England he wrote again and again about his accomplishment.

Byron and Hobhouse visited Constantinople together but parted company afterward, with Hobhouse returning to England in July 1810. Byron, short of money, returned to Athens rather than going home. He settled in a Capuchin religious house, where he studied Italian. He enjoyed the company of boys at its school and fellow travelers who roomed there. He wrote to Hobhouse of being entertained by "several Albanian women washing in the 'Giardino,' whose hours of relaxation are spent in running pins into Fletcher's backside." (Marchand, 254)

But in between such entertaining moments, Byron found time to muse, write poetry, and indulge in intrigues. It may have been one of these that ended in his rescuing a Turkish girl sentenced to death for immoral behavior. Byron came upon a crowd watching her, wrapped in a sack and about to be thrown into the sea. Byron stopped the soldiers at gunpoint, then cajoled and bribed the Turkish governor to let the girl leave Athens. He later used this incident in *The Giaour*.

In fact, after the steady Hobhouse left, Byron lived a much wilder life. He contracted a sexually transmitted disease and suffered other health problems. These included a bout with fever, then a relapse. Still, when he survived, Byron felt so pleased that he had lost weight he put himself on a regimen of vinegar, water, and rice.

When he received more bad financial news from Hanson, Byron responded that nothing could make him sell Newstead. He sent Fletcher home but put off his own return to England.

Although Mrs. Spencer Smith kept her part of their tryst in Malta, when the time came, Byron did not. During his last months in Athens, he wrote a great deal, including another satire about his contemporaries entitled "Hints from Horace." A second poem, "The Curse of Minerva," attacked Lord Elgin for robbing Greece of its cultural treasures.

When he finally surrendered to financial realities, Byron parted reluctantly from English, French, Greek, and Turkish friends in Athens. He did not leave everything behind, though. When he boarded his ship, the *Hydra*, at Piraius, "four ancient Athenian skulls, dug out of sarcophagi—a phial of Attic hemlock—four live tortoises—a greyhound ... two live Greek servants, one an Athenian, t'other a *Yaniote*, who can speak nothing but Romaic and Italian" (Marchand, 270–271) sailed with him. Ironically, the last major shipment of Lord Elgin's marbles made part of the cargo as well.

Byron, now a citizen of the world, set foot in Portsmouth, England, two years and twelve days after he sailed from English shores. Travel had broadened his views and changed him greatly. He had mingled with people of varied cultures. He especially admired the fatalism of Islam as he learned it from the Turks. And, as Andre Maurois writes, "Henceforth he would know that, if things went askew with him in England, a fortnight of sea would bring him to white islands beneath a sky for ever blue." (Maurois, 145)

However, his immediate concerns involved *Childe Harold*. Byron had given his friend Dallas the copyright, believing no gentleman should write for money. While Dallas negotiated with publishers, Byron tried to sort out his business interests with Hanson.

News arrived that Catherine was seriously ill at Newstead. Byron learned of her death before he could leave London. At Newstead, deep grief eclipsed memories of his old quarrels with his mother. Even before Catherine's burial, Byron learned that his old

Cambridge friend Matthews had drowned. Next a third friend from Harrow died, and finally, his beloved Edleston. His poem, "To Thyrza," expressed his grief for that loss. Byron felt alone and desolate. But there was still Augusta, who sent him a touching letter of sympathy. He invited her to visit him.

Meanwhile, Dallas, who had found a potential publisher for *Childe Harold*, pressured Byron to change lines he felt were too freethinking with regard to religion. Byron responded, "I will have nothing to do with your immortality; we are miserable enough in this life, without the absurdity of speculating on another ... let me live, well if possible, and die without pain. The rest is with God...." (Marchand, 291) In the end, he agreed to minor changes but held firm to keeping most lines as originally written.

Byron remained at Newstead mourning his losses. Eventually, however, a new mistress, his varied menagerie, hunts on his estate, and the new habit of chewing tobacco to ward off hunger pangs signaled improved spirits. He acted the part of lord of the manor when he "issued an edict for the abolition of caps; no hair to be cut on any pretext; stays permitted, but not too low before; full uniform always in the evening." (Drinkwater, 168)

Byron journeyed to London, with a bittersweet stop at Cambridge, where he mourned Edleston. In London, he made welcome new friends of the Irish poet Thomas Moore and the English poet Samuel Rogers.

After a return stay at Newstead, he moved to London and on January 15, 1812, took his seat in the House of Lords for its parliamentary session. He deliberated on a subject for his first speech. Events in Nottingham provided the answer. Weavers there had been replaced by modern machinery. They rioted in protest, breaking into houses and smashing the manufacturing frames that had displaced them. The Tory riot bill specified death as the penalty for frame breakers.

Byron passionately opposed the bill. He blamed the poverty of the weavers not only on foreign wars, but also on emerging industrialism. He stated, "I have been in some of the most oppressed provinces of Turkey; but never, under the most despotic of infidel governments, did I behold such squalid wretchedness as I have seen since my return, in the very heart of a Christian country." (Untermeyer, 387–388) Although the bill passed, Byron's eloquent opposition met with praise from Whigs and Tories alike.

But his reputation soared with the publication, on March 10, 1812, of *Childe Harold's Pilgrimage*. Byron would say that he "awoke one morning and found [himself] famous." (Untermeyer, 388) Biographer John Drinkwater says, "[T]he public was not only ready for the new design of his poetry; it found in his mood something of the skepticism and disillusion that were gathering across Europe upon the closing scenes of Napoleon's adventures." (Drinkwater, 182) *Childe Harold* was a blend of autobiography, history, politics, and philosophy.

Its autobiographical aspects proved as exciting to London society as the noble young poet did himself. He was young, but had traveled to remote lands; his features resembled a Greek statue; he had the call to sympathy of a lame foot; he could be funny; and he had already impressed the House of Lords. The Duchess of Devonshire said the men were jealous of him, "the women of each other." (Maurois, 177) London had a bad case of Byronic fever. After meeting the charismatic poet and watching women fawn over him, one young woman, Lady Caroline Lamb, wrote prophetically in her diary, "Mad, bad, and dangerous to know." (Maurois, 178)

OBJECTS OF LOVE

Byron, the debt-ridden aristocrat with no connections, enjoyed the effect he now created on noblewomen such as Caroline Lamb. According to biographer Andre Maurois, "[H]e kept trying the fascinating power of his famous 'underlook.'" (Maurois, 176) This intense gaze through the poet's long lashes caused many a titled heart to flutter.

But none beat with the passion of the uninhibited Lady Caroline Ponsonby Lamb's. Two days after writing her first words about the most talked about man in London, she added, "That beautiful pale face is my fate." (Maurois, 178) Tired of the superficial world of the mannered aristocracy, she had found her sexual and intellectual ideal.

If Byron captivated Caroline, she intrigued him at least as much. In England he had known only country girls, prostitutes, and servants. Lionized by society, with more invitations than he could accept, he still felt awkward in the company of aristocrats who had known each other's families since childhood. The waltz had become the rage and, since his foot prevented dancing, added to his sense of not fitting in despite his rank.

Byron's feelings about women in general were contradictory. Part of him viewed women as animals to be used for pleasure, part searched for an object to love, part wanted excitement, and part yearned for a mother figure. Byron needed love in some form. Throughout his life he would form passionate attachments to boys, but women maintained a dominant allure. He wrote in his journal, "There is something very softening in the presence of a woman—some strange influence, even if one is not in love with them—which I cannot account for, having no very high opinion of the sex. But yet I always feel in better humor with myself, and everything else, if there is a woman within ken." (Drinkwater, 204)

The married Caroline Lamb belonged to a privileged world of aristocrats who believed themselves entitled to live by their own social rules. If public scenes and scandals were avoided, extra-marital liaisons were commonly accepted among her peers. Well educated, able to read French and Italian by age five, Caroline had lived abroad, wrote, sketched, and knew how to forge signatures. She was a delicate, small woman whose only living child, a son, was epileptic. Her moods careened so that some biographers think she suffered from manic depression. (Indeed, some speculate the same about Byron.) Her friends nicknamed her Sprite, Ariel, Squirrel, and Cherubina. This last reflected her tendency to dress in boys' clothes. During their affair and afterwards, she disguised herself as a page to enter Byron's rooms.

They met in May, and the affair was passionate, meteoric, and stormy. Letters flew between their residences. At one point, Hobhouse stepped in to prevent them from eloping. Byron tired of Caroline's reckless lack of discretion by September. Her feelings for him remained a lifelong, consuming obsession. Biographer Margot Strickland quotes Caroline in later life writing of "that dear, that angel, that misguided and misguiding Byron, whom I adore, although he left that dreadful legacy on me, my memory." (Strickland, 55)

She had some right to call him misguiding; at times he turned cruel. He attended events to which she was not invited while she hovered outside. Once, when he spoke coldly to her at a party, she grabbed a knife and cut herself. However, when her mother, husband, and mother-in-law persuaded her to go to Ireland in an attempt to end such scenes, Byron wept as he said farewell.

She wrote from Ireland, and he answered, "I was and am yours freely and most entirely, to obey, to honour, to love—and fly with you when, where and how yourself *might* and may determine." (Strickland, 55) In the same letter he used the words, "When I quit you, or rather you, from a sense of duty to your husband and mother, quit me...." (Drinkwater, 211)

A frantic Caroline could hardly be blamed for clinging to hopes of their being a couple again. When that hope withered, she wrote a bitter novel, *Glenarvin*, the main character a thinly disguised Byron.

Another prominent noblewoman would never be his lover, but would influence his relationships with others. She was Caroline Lamb's mother-in-law and his future wife's aunt, Lady Melbourne. Lady Melbourne was sixty-two when they began a frank correspondence. Byron shared everything with her regarding his affairs. Lady Melbourne accepted the task when he asked her to direct him in his personal life.

With a house near Westminster, she was a politically powerful hostess and a former mistress of the Prince of Wales. Byron admired her intellect and, of course, found a mother substitute and social guide in this sophisticated, still attractive woman. Byron wrote, "If she had been a few years younger, what a fool she would have made of me." (Strickland, 108)

It was at Melbourne House on the morning of March 25, 1812, that Byron met Annabella Milbanke, Lady Melbourne's niece. Biographer Thomas Medwin quoted the superstitious Byron later as saying, "It was a fatal day; and I remember that in going upstairs I stumbled, and remarked to Moore, who accompanied me, that it was a bad omen. I ought to have taken the warning." (Marchand, 331)

Twenty-year-old Annabella was the only child of doting parents, who raised her in their house at Seaham in Durham. Educated at home, the dark-haired girl had an analytical mind with knowledge of mathematics, philosophy, and classical literature. She caught the interest of several eligible young men during that London season with her good figure and reserved manner.

Annabella's first journal entry about Byron differed from Caroline Lamb's: "His mouth continually betrays the acrimony of his spirit. He tried to control his natural sarcasm and vehemence as much as he could, in order not to offend; but at times his lips thickened with disdain, and his eyes rolled impatiently." (Marchand, 333) She wrote to her mother that rumors of his being an infidel were probably true, but "his poem sufficiently proves that he *can* feel nobly, but he has discouraged his own goodness...." (Marchand, 368)

Lady Melbourne nurtured Byron's interest in her niece. If he married Annabella he would be permanently and publicly finished with Caroline, have a way out of debt, as she was an heiress, and be able to truly call Lady Melbourne his aunt. Lady Melbourne asked Annabella what qualities she desired in a husband. Her prim, serious niece enclosed a list that seemed to describe Byron's exact opposite. Unfortunately, in spite of knowing them both so well, Lady Melbourne forged ahead, encouraging the marriage of opposites.

Byron proposed in October, but sensible Annabella turned him down. Although stung by the rejection, Byron eventually wrote to Lady Melbourne, "My principal inducement was the tie to yourself, which I confess would have delighted me," adding, "I congratulate A and myself on our mutual escape. That would have been but a cold *collation*, and I prefer hot dinners." (Strickland, 111) He consoled himself in the arms of a happily married Italian opera singer.

Within months, Byron found a deeper love interest in Jane Elizabeth Scott, Countess of Oxford. She was a recruiter for the Hampton Club, a group of liberal reformers who elected Byron to their membership. She and her husband had an open marriage, and her several children were referred to as the Harleian Miscellany, since they may have all had different fathers. She was forty when the twenty-four-year old Byron met her. She invited him to the Oxfords' country home at Eywood.

Whereas Caroline was hysterical, Lady Oxford was a serene beauty; Byron became her devoted lover. He basked in being part of her family life, playing and reading with her children. At one point he imagined marrying her lovely eleven-year-old daughter in years to come. When Caroline not only wrote to Byron, but sent a tirade to Lady Oxford, Byron had had enough. He wrote back that he was now attached to another. Lady Oxford's seal on the letter left no doubt about his new love's identity. Caroline fell ill after reading his words but published them later in *Glenarvin*.

Back in England, Caroline asked him to return her letters. At her country home in Brocket, she dressed a group of little girls in white and had them dance around a great bonfire while she burned effigies of Byron and copies of his letters as a page boy read lines she had composed. She would later have her servants' liveries adorned with buttons that read "Ne Crede Byron" (Don't trust Byron).

Lady Oxford and Byron each returned to London where they were part of the inner circle of the Princess of Wales. At Lady Oxford's urging Byron tried a half-hearted return to politics, but he realized soon that he was not destined for brilliance in parliament. He toyed with the idea of traveling abroad with the Oxfords but in the end lacked the necessary money.

His finances continued in serious trouble. To erase longstanding, heavy debts he finally agreed to sell Newstead. The whole estate of 3,200 acres went on the market. Byron set 120,000 pounds as a minimum price, and the loyal Hobhouse, who had only one pound, one shilling, and a sixpence to his name, arrived and nervously bid to drive up competing offers at the auction. In the end, Byron accepted no bids, but the next day he sold everything to Thomas Claughton. Claughton almost immediately went into default, adding to Byron's frustrations.

Through all this, Byron continued to write, usually in the quiet hours when others slept. In addition to his poems, he wrote an address for the opening of the newly rebuilt Drury Lane Theatre. He also tossed off some anonymous satires about the king—an activity still considered treason in 1813. In "The Waltz," he bitterly lampooned the dance he resented and took daring potshots at "princely paunches." But he triumphed again with the first of his works with eastern themes. He started *The Giaour* in late 1812 and published its first version in May 1813.

During a visit to London when Lady Oxford remained at Eywood, Byron visited Leigh Hunt in prison. Hunt was a hero to liberals, having been jailed for libeling the Prince Regent. Byron loaned Hunt books, and Hunt proudly wrote to his wife that he believed they would become friends. Byron also met the celebrated literary lioness of Europe, Madame de Staël, but they did not become friends. Byron disliked aggressively intellectual women.

Lady Oxford sailed out of Byron's life with her husband on June 28, 1813. Byron confessed to Lady Melbourne that he felt more "Carolinish" about her than he had expected. (Marchand, 394) He was not there to see Lady Oxford off because Augusta suddenly arrived in London, financially ruined, thanks mainly to her husband's addiction to gambling, especially on horse races.

The grown brother and sister recognized that each had found a soul mate. Augusta looked like Byron: similar classic features and coloring, a soft and voluptuous figure. She also possessed his wicked sense of humor. Both were shy in public, but at ease and like-minded with each other. He was her "Baby Byron," and she was his silly, funny "Goose." Within weeks they became lovers. They attended London plays and social events as a twosome.

On August 5, 1813, Byron wrote to Lady Melbourne that his sister would be going abroad with him. Never good at keeping secrets, he wrote letters that hinted at incest but did not name it directly. Sometime in late August he confessed to the nature of their relationship and managed to dismay even the worldly Lady Melbourne, who strongly argued against their travel plans. Gothic novels of the time often used incest as a theme, but confronting it in real life was different from reading fiction.

Why would Byron and Augusta let their relationship become sexual? They understood each other, but beyond this Byron was fascinated by sin as well as new sensations. According to author Leslie Marchand, Augusta was "[a]moral as a rabbit and silly as a goose." (Marchand, 404) She quoted Scripture but failed to take sin, or much else, too seriously.

Meanwhile, Annabella, bored at Seaham and remembering the romantic poet, wrote Byron a long letter. Byron wrote a warm, flattering answer. Neither informed Lady Melbourne of their renewed correspondence. Byron did tell his friend Medwin, "The tenor of her letter was, that although she could not love me, she desired my friendship. Friendship is a dangerous word for young ladies; it is Love full-fledged, and waiting for a fine day to fly." (Marchand, 407)

Life grew more complicated. He visited Augusta at her home at Six Mile Bottom in September, and it apparently did not go well. A visit to his friend Webster later that month resulted in a complicated flirtation with Webster's wife, Lady Frances. Correspondence with Annabella continued, but she tended to write naïve sermons in the misguided belief that she might tame and reform the doomed, moody libertine.

Annabella, whom Byron dubbed the "Princess of Parallelograms," had no idea of Byron's real concerns. His relationship with Augusta filled his guilt-ridden thoughts. He began *The Bride of Abydos*, with a theme of incest. He followed it in January 1814 with *The Corsair*, a second and obviously autobiographical eastern tale with an anguished hero.

Augusta became pregnant; the timing made it almost certain that the child was Byron's and not her husband's. In January, Byron and Augusta went to Newstead together, cozily snowbound. In spite of Lady Melbourne's disapproval, Byron wrote of his contentment, saying, "[w]e never yawn nor disagree ..." (Marchand, 433) They stayed together until February 6, 1813, delighted by the news that *The Corsair* had become a bestseller.

Byron and Augusta's daughter Elizabeth Medora was born at Six Mile Bottom on April 15, 1813. Lady Melbourne asked Byron whether the dangers of his and Augusta's affair were worthwhile. He responded, "Oh! But it is 'worth while,' I can't tell you why, and it is *not* an 'Ape.'" (Marchand, 466) He was referring to a medieval belief that children who were the products of incest would be monsters. He did promise Lady Melbourne that he would now reform. Marriage to a virtuous woman seemed to be the best way to achieve this.

The letters to and from Annabella had developed into a wary courtship dance. On March 15, 1814, he noted in his journal, "A letter from *Bella*, which I answered. I shall be in love with her again if I don't take care." (Marchand, 442) Augusta and Lady Melbourne both encouraged him to pursue marriage.

On September 9, he sent a second proposal to Annabella from Newstead. Nine days later, Byron was having dinner when the gardener brought in his mother's lost wedding ring. The letter from Annabella arrived during the same meal. Byron told Augusta, who was visiting, that if Annabella's answer was "yes," they would be married with the ring. Her answer was "yes," and they were.

THE STORMIEST HOUR

Even before they became engaged, Byron wrote of Annabella, "She is much too good for a fallen spirit to know, and I should like her more if she were less perfect." (Untermeyer, 391) When she was forty,

Annabella wrote, "[n]ot to see things as they are is then my great intellectual defect." (Praz, 48) Her analysis was sadly accurate. By the time Annabella accepted Byron's proposal she was blindly in love. The strait-laced, pious girl over-confidently believed she could save her fiancé's lost soul. Byron himself was ambivalent and nervous about the engagement. He delayed going to meet her family at Seaham until November 2. An embarrassed Annabella finally persuaded him to come by hinting that her parents were losing their patience.

He arrived with no ring or presents. When they met, Byron stood unmoving by the fireplace as Annabella walked toward him. He awkwardly kissed her extended hand and murmured that they had not seen each other for a long time. Flustered, she rushed out of the room to find her mother and father.

The next day he slept late, and then they walked together by the cold North Sea. Byron wrote to Lady Melbourne that there was tension: "However, the die is cast; neither party can recede; the lawyers are here—mine and all—and I presume, the parchment once scribbled, I shall become Lord Annabella." (Marchand, 490–491)

In spite of easily reaching a prenuptial settlement, the couple were ill at ease. After Byron announced, "If you had married me two years ago, you would have spared me what I can never get over," (Marchand, 492) a mystified Annabella offered to end the engagement. He said no, but still had doubts. When he turned to physical caresses, Annabella, afraid of succumbing to her passions before she was a properly married woman, sent him back to London.

Byron absolutely refused to be married in a church, so they asked for special permission from the Archbishop of Canterbury to be married where they chose. The Milbankes set the date for a private ceremony at Seaham.

Even with the news that the wedding cake was baked, Byron procrastinated about leaving London again. When Claughton failed to purchase Newstead, Byron offered to postpone the wedding indefinitely. Finally, he began the journey, stopping for Christmas at Six Mile Bottom. There he wrote a letter to Annabella breaking off the engagement, but Augusta, eager to save their reputations, talked him out of mailing it.

He picked up Hobhouse, his best man, at Cambridge. They moved on, Hobhouse noting in his diary, "The bridegroom more and more less impatient." (Marchand, 503)

They arrived on December 30. Hobhouse liked Annabella, although he did not see her as beautiful. On New Year's Eve moods lightened with a mock marriage ceremony, Hobhouse acting as the bride. January 1 was a sober, quiet day. The wedding took place in the drawing room the next morning, where kneeling mats had been laid down for the bride and groom. Annabella wore a simple white muslin gown, and Byron wore black.

Hobhouse remembered that Byron stammered a little on starting his vows and threw Hobhouse an ironic half-smile at the part about endowing Annabella with all his worldly goods. The ceremony started at 10:30 a.m. and ended by 11:00. There was no reception. When they left for their honeymoon, Annabella traveled in an outfit of grey satin trimmed in white fur.

Hobhouse ended his journal entry about the wedding, "Of my dearest friend I took a melancholy leave. He was unwilling to leave my hand and I had hold of his out of the window when the carriage drove off." (Marchand, 506)

They were to spend their "treaclemoon," (Marchand, 518) as Byron called it, at Halnaby Hall, Annabella's uncle's house in Yorkshire, forty miles away. As the carriage rolled through the wintry landscape, Annabella's nightmare began. Byron kept silent for a while, then burst into an Albanian dirge. Annabella and her mother had predicted the marriage would end in separation. When they finally stopped, Byron limped off into the night, leaving Annabella to face servants greeting them with flaming torches.

Byron returned, and Moore read in Byron's memoirs that he "had Lady B. on the sofa before dinner on the day of their marriage." (Marchand, 510) Byron said that he preferred sleeping alone, but Annabella could join him if she wanted to—one woman being as good as another. When he woke in his four-poster bed, firelight glowing through red curtains, his bride beside him, Byron cried out, believing himself in hell.

Annabella's husband was not rational. When a pseudo-love letter arrived from Augusta, he taunted Annabella by reading it aloud. He saw that she had wrapped a black ribbon around his mother's ring to make it fit and scolded her in superstitious horror. He had read her list of qualities for a husband and now teased her with stories of insanity that ran through his family. He hinted at past passions and misbehavior of every sort. Annabella tried to stay calm and affectionate but at one point burst out to her maid, "I am sure there has been something dreadful between him and his sister!" (Strickland, 75)

Nights became a torment to Byron, who sometimes paced with loaded pistols. Once, Annabella called him back to bed, laying her head on his chest. In a rare, gentle moment, he said, "You should have a softer pillow than my heart." She wondered back which would break first, "yours or mine." (Strickland, 76)

During some peaceful domestic hours they read together in the library. He nicknamed her Pippin, or Pip, because of her round face. She called him "Dear Duck." Byron worked on a series of poems with themes from the Old Testament, *Hebrew Melodies*. Around this time he also began "Parisina," which dealt with the charged theme of incest. The new Lady Byron copied them by hand for her husband. In spite of how he often taunted her in person, he praised her in letters to friends.

She managed to keep an outward calm and affection no matter how he mistreated her. Sometimes that soothed him, but often it irritated him and he tortured her with more insults and ravings. He also played on her habit of taking everything he said, including threats against their future children, literally.

They left Halnaby to return to Seaham for Byron's birthday. As they rode, he turned to Annabella and said, "I think you now know pretty well which subjects to avoid." (Marchand, 517) At Seaham, Byron's behavior improved as he took part in family pastimes even though he complained in letters to friends of being bored. After six weeks, the newlyweds left for Six Mile Bottom. Biographer Margot Strickland writes, "The gentilities of the Milbanke family were left behind and a warm, untidy, cheerfully sinning aristocratic household awaited...." (Strickland, 77)

At his sister's house, Byron drank heavily. He relentlessly abused both women, Augusta for having been his lover, Annabella for marrying a man who preferred his own sister. When Annabella admired Medora, Byron announced, "You know that is my child." (Strickland, 77) He insisted Annabella go to bed alone at night while he stayed up with Augusta, telling his wife, "We don't want *you*, my charmer." (Marchand, 524)

He ordered two gold brooches with his and Augusta's hair enclosed and their signature crosses engraved in the gold. Even so, the two women grew closer, mutually wanting to return Byron to sane behavior, both for their benefit and his. By the time the Byrons left Augusta on March 28 for their new home in London, Lady Byron was pregnant. Byron turned temporarily kinder in London. He enjoyed the company of old friends and attended to literary and financial concerns. Then Annabella invited Augusta to visit.

Augusta had just that year been appointed as a Woman of the Bedchamber to the seventy-one-year-old Queen Charlotte, so she would be spending periods of time in London in any case. However, Byron himself called Annabella foolish for inviting his sister to their home. Perhaps Annabella hoped to reshape their family dynamics, but that did not happen. Byron once again became so irritable and cruel that it was a relief for Annabella when she had to leave to visit a dying uncle. When Augusta went back to Six Mile Bottom, Byron followed her. After she refused to take up their old affair, he angrily returned to London.

His concerns there included becoming a member of the subcommittee of management of the Drury Lane Theater. He socialized with the influential men who served with him and with the seductive actresses. He had an indiscreet affair with an actress named Susan Boyce. He needled Annabella about his relationships with actresses, once pretending remorse and then bursting into laughter. He also made a will leaving everything to Augusta. Annabella confided to her sister-in-law that she now understood that her difficult husband's greatest misfortune was his constant *"passion* for *excitement."* (Strickland, 24)

When the sale of Newstead failed and Annabella's uncle left most of his money to others, their financial problems reached crisis level. A bailiff moved into the house to protect the interests of creditors. Byron had to sell his beloved library to pay part of his debts. He took his misery out on Annabella, who begged Augusta to return. Augusta, Annabella's maid, and Fletcher tried their best to protect Annabella, actually fearing that Byron's mental abuse might turn physical.

The couple's daughter was born on December 10, 1815; they named her Augusta Ada. Stories circulated later that while Annabella was in labor, Byron popped corks against the ceiling of the room below her. He denied that, but, certainly did other hurtful things. During one frenzied rage on January 3, 1816, he suggested they break up the household in London. He planned to send Annabella to her parents, while he would follow at some unspecified date. On January 6, he wrote his wife a cold note that read in part, "When you are disposed to leave London it would be convenient that a day should be fixed ... the child will of course accompany you." (Strickland, 79)

Annabella agreed to go, but before she did she searched Byron's belongings for evidence to support her theory that he was mentally ill. She called on Drs. Baillie and Le Mann, asking that Dr. Baillie examine Byron to confirm insanity. She talked to Hanson, expressing a fear that her husband might commit suicide. Byron's cousin, George Anson Byron, who was staying with them and worried about Annabella's safety, finally persuaded her to leave.

Augusta witnessed a cool parting between husband and wife on January 14. Byron did not rise in time to see Annabella off the next morning. She remembered her feelings as she passed his room. "There was a large mat on which his Newfoundland dog used to lie. For a moment I was tempted to throw myself on it, and wait at all hazards, but it was only a moment—and I passed on. That was our parting." (Marchand, 562)

Doctors Baillie and Le Mann advised Annabella to write affectionate, cheerful letters to Byron from the country. Their plan was that he would follow her; the doctors thought he might need to be under medical supervision. She followed their advice, but their final diagnosis was not insanity. By then Annabella had told her outraged parents how Byron behaved toward her. Robbed of being able to excuse him because of madness, his miserable wife agreed when her mother and father insisted she obtain a deed of separation.

The letter from the Milbankes' lawyer informing Byron of his wife's decision stunned him. He wrote Annabella, begging her to think of happier times. He wrote the sentimental poem, "Fare Thee Well," expressing his sorrow and self-pity. She, however, was skeptical of his eleventh-hour remorse and at one point wrote him, "It is unhappily your disposition to consider what you have as worthless— what you have *lost* as invaluable." (Strickland, 83)

Stories about the separation and its causes, known by now to doctors, lawyers, servants, and others, swept through London. Byron and Augusta were outcasts. Rumors of their incest, his bisexuality, and his many mistresses flew through society's drawing rooms. When Lady Jersey defied the social climate and invited them to a party, other guests left the rooms they entered.

It was more than just his questionable behavior that caused Byron to be ostracized. He had written daring political verses that made him unpopular. He favored Catholic Emancipation and defended the Nottingham frame-breakers. He admired Napoleon but openly criticized the Duke of Wellington along with the English and French monarchies. Tories attacked him, and his own Whig Party did nothing. He had gone too far. As author Strickland writes, "The young poet was seen as a socially, politically and morally disturbing influence whose ideas, if carried to their logical conclusion, would result in the total disintegration of society...." (Strickland, 82)

Byron decided to leave England. Augusta visited him on Easter Sunday, April 14, to say a tearful goodbye. After she had gone, Byron wrote to Annabella asking her to be kind to his sister if anything should happen to him. Later, under Annabella's interrogation, Augusta apparently admitted that incest had occurred, but always maintained it stopped after Byron's marriage. Augusta kept her apartments at St. James Palace, but she and her reputation never fully recovered.

By the time he left England, Byron had stopped feeling sentimental about his "Mathematical Media." (Strickland, 84) He expressed his bitterness when he added four lines in the margin of the deed of separation he signed two days before sailing:

> A year ago, you swore, fond she!
> "To love, to honour," and so forth:
> Such was the vow you pledged to me,
> And here's exactly what it's worth.
> (Maurois, 329)

In 1818, after hearing that Annabella's lawyer for the separation had killed himself in grief over his own wife's death, Byron wrote bitterly to Annabella: "This Man little thought, when he was lacerating my heart according to law, while he was poisoning my life at it's sources ... that a domestic affliction would lay him in the earth with the meanest of malefactors...." (Marchand, 759)

During his preparations for departure, Byron had a carriage made, an elaborate copy of one owned by Napoleon; he planned to take it to Europe. He would also take Fletcher and a young doctor,

John William Polidori, who hoped to write a travel diary. A few loyal friends, including Hobhouse, Scrope Davies, Hanson, Douglas Kinnaird, and Leigh Hunt, continued to drink and dine with Byron in London in spite of his disgrace. He left the house at Piccadilly on April 24, 1816, bound for Dover. As soon as the carriage rolled away, bailiffs arrived to seize everything, including Byron's pet squirrel.

People in Dover were curious to have a look at the scandalous poet. Ladies disguised themselves as chambermaids for the appearance of an excuse to loiter in the hallways of his inn.

On the morning of April 25, Byron set sail on the first stage of his journey to Switzerland. He wrote a quick poetic farewell to his friend Tom Moore. Its last lines read:

> Here's a sigh to those who love me,
> And a smile to those who hate;
> And whatever sky's above me,
> Here's a heart for every fate!
> (Maurois, 331)

Byron would never see England again.

POET IN EXILE

Byron behaved as his usual self when he reached his inn in Ostend, Belgium. According to Polidori, Byron "fell like a thunderbolt upon the chambermaid." (Marchand, 610) He went on to Brussels, then visited the battlefield of Waterloo, hunting for bones. Again true to old habits, he and Polidori carved their names in the chapel at Hougoumont.

Because of Byron's liberal politics, he was not allowed into France, so the two men entered Switzerland through the Rhine Valley. Byron wrote poetic descriptions of all he saw to Augusta, unaware that Annabella was plaguing his sister with her need for confession and soul-saving.

On May 25, 1816, the travelers arrived at Dejean's hotel on Lake Geneva. When he registered, Byron entered his age as "100." (Maurois, 339) A few days earlier, Claire Clarinmont, Byron's last English lover, had stayed there with her stepsister, Mary Godwin, the mistress and future wife of the poet Percy Bysshe Shelley. Although Claire was carrying his child, Byron had cooled toward her by the time he sailed from England. She had always been the pursuer. He reluctantly agreed to see her in Switzerland.

When he arrived, she introduced the two poets. Byron rented the lakeside Villa Diodati, and the Shelleys stayed in a smaller house in the vineyards below. Shelley and Byron formed a close friendship based on liberal sympathies, reading the revolutionary ideas of Rousseau, as well as Voltaire, Gibbon, and others. The four spent many evenings together. Mary, Byron, and Shelley wrote while Claire copied Byron's works. As a result of their deciding that each should write a ghost story, Mary wrote her famous novel *Frankenstein*. The two couples, along with Polidori, also rowed on Lake Geneva in the evenings.

Claire and Byron continued as lovers, although he mostly only tolerated her. He wrote to Augusta, "I could not exactly play the stoic with a woman who had scrambled eight hundred miles to unphilosophize me." (Strickland, 124)

Byron began to work on *Childe Harold* again. On a sightseeing tour with Shelley, he visited Chillon Castle and carved his name in its dungeon. When bad weather kept them indoors for two days just afterward, Byron composed *The Prisoner of Chillon* about a revolutionary figure whose mind remains free even while he is chained.

Late summer arrived. To Byron's relief, the Shelleys took Claire back to England in July to wait for her baby's birth. In August, Hobhouse and Scrope Davies arrived. Hobhouse happily wrote to Augusta that Byron was living quietly and seemed calm. The three old friends set off with Polidori for Alpine touring. Matthew Lewis visited as well and introduced Byron to a translation of *Faust*. The story of the man who made a bargain with the devil, heard in the rugged grandeur of the Alps, inspired Byron's dark, dramatic poem *Manfred*.

He was by now a serious poet. Exile and Shelley had worked their influence. Soothed by solitude and nature, stimulated by Shelley's intellect, Byron had also written "The Dream," dealing with his love for Mary Ann Chaworth, and "Epistle to Augusta." Another writer's work featured Byron's past, too. Madame de Staël, now a neighbor in Switzerland, told him about the publication of Caroline Lamb's novel *Glenarvin*. When he finally read it, he wrote to Moore,

"As for the likeness, the picture can't be good—I did not sit long enough." (Marchand, 642)

By October, Byron tired of being stared at by curious English tourists. He also wanted a warmer place to spend the winter. He and Hobhouse left Diodati together, their destination, Milan. Once there, Byron immediately found himself part of the Italian liberal intelligentsia. He went to the opera and ballet and held discussions with Greek expatriates and Italian rebels.

These were dangerous contacts. When Napoleon met defeat, the Congress of Vienna divided Europe into sections. Austria now ruled the provinces of Lombardy and Venice using police power to control the unhappy Italians.

On November 4, 1816, Byron and Hobhouse left Milan for Venice, which suited Byron. Mindful as always of his limp, he liked the idea of gliding over the water in gondol's instead of walking. And Byron's Venetian life included a new mistress. Marianna Segati was the twenty-two-year-old wife of his landlord, an Italian draper whose shops were below Byron's rooms.

Byron studied Armenian during the day, working with Father Pascal Aucher to finish an English-Armenian grammar. Byron tackled the task because, he wrote, "I found that my mind wanted something craggy to break upon...." (Maurois, 378) He also went riding on the Lido with Marianna but was a libertine at night, especially during the naughty season of Carnival just before Lent.

He found something close to contentment. He wrote that he had "books—a decent establishment—a fine country—a language which I prefer—most of the amusements and conveniences of life—as much of society as I choose to take ... and would never ever willingly dwell in the 'tight little Island' again." (Maurois, 379–380) Only Augusta's subdued responses to his ardent letters disturbed him. She wrote that if he did return to England they could not meet intimately.

On January 12, 1817, Byron and Claire's daughter, Allegra, was born. Knowing he would probably never have a relationship with Ada, he agreed to raise Allegra himself. He gave Claire permission to see her from time to time so long as Byron and Claire would have no direct contact. Shelley would be their go-between. Claire agreed apprehensively, but she believed Byron's rank and fame would benefit their daughter.

After his excesses during Carnival, Byron's health gave way, and in February he wrote the gentle lyric "So We'll Go No More A' Roving" to Marianna. He seemed to be settling down.

Most of all, he focused on writing poetry. In two and a half years, between October 1816 and July 1819, Byron wrote almost 9,000 lines. These included the final version of the dramatic *Manfred*, written during a stay in Rome. In it, his own view of hell moved from the fiery vision of his Calvinist childhood lessons to the hell that a man like the poet could create within himself. He finished more *Childe Harold* at a villa at La Mira, a former convent he took for the summer with Hobhouse and Marianna as guests.

Then he discovered the poetic satiric form that led to *Beppo*, written in October of 1817. During the next year, Byron began his epic freewheeling *Don Juan* in the *Beppo* style. *Don Juan* was his greatest work. He would continue adding new cantos to it until his death, the public always eager to read them.

Still, his personal life lacked direction. He had tired of Marianna by this time. He drifted into promiscuity with lower and middle class Italian women and contracted gonorrhea. Even so, he prepared to bring Allegra into his newly leased home, the Mocenigo Palace on the Grand Canal.

In September 1817, he met Margarita Cogni, known as La Fornarina (the furnace). She was a wild, fiercely passionate woman married to a butcher. La Fornarina was illiterate but opened Byron's letters in jealous fits after she moved in uninvited, claiming her place as the new housekeeper. In that capacity she cut his bills in half and terrorized his household. When Byron finally ordered her to leave, she hysterically threw herself into the canal, but she was rescued and eventually left Byron alone.

Even without La Fornarina, Byron's household and lifestyle remained eccentric. He swam in the canal, rode horses on the Lido, kept Allegra with him, studied Armenian, and wrote poetry. His menagerie included two monkeys, a fox, a wolf, dogs, and a civet cat. At times he added two cats, a hawk, and a crow. He felt strongly that England held little more for him. When Lady Melbourne died in April 1818, he wrote to his publisher, "There is one link less between England and myself." (Maurois, 397) He decided to sell Newstead, pay his debts, and live abroad. One step toward security was that he decided to accept money for his writing. The London publisher John Murray bought copyrights for his works and paid him well for some time.

In spite of Byron's decision to stay in Italy, he felt a lack of purpose. He could be playful, but in a serious moment he wrote to Moore, "I have not the least idea where I am going, nor what I am to do." (Drinkwater, 287)

Then, in April 1819, he became acquainted with Teresa, Countess Guiccioli. They had met three days after her marriage a year ago and now saw each other again at a party in Venice. From that evening on they were constantly together, until the young wife was taken by her elderly, rather sinister husband to their home in Ravenna. When Teresa fell ill her husband sent for Byron, who nursed her back to health, remaining with her in the role of "cavalier servente."

Under the Italian social code, a wife could take a lover who would be at her service at all times, while her husband pretended not to notice that a sexual relationship existed as part of their friendship. Byron had never wanted to participate in what Marchand describes as the "fan and shawl carrying traditions of the cult," (Marchand, 778) but he loved Teresa as much as he could love any woman.

She was auburn-haired with a lovely bust and shoulders, only nineteen, well educated, and like Augusta she had a fine sense of the ridiculous. She was the only woman who could make Byron jealous. She calmed, teased, pleased, and exasperated him. She was not boring. When they went riding, he complained, "She can't guide her horse ... he runs after mine and tries to bite him, and then she begins screaming." (Strickland, 143)

In August 1819, Count Guiccioli took Teresa to Bologna. He had cultivated Byron's friendship and now, in a not so subtle move, asked his wife's lover to have him appointed British vice-consul at Ravenna. Byron tried without success, but he loaned the count large sums of money upon request.

Byron and Teresa were allowed to stay by themselves for a time at La Mira. Even then, the romantic Teresa was careful to be a bit elusive, never eating in Byron's presence and spending considerable time in her own rooms. When Allegra came to stay, Teresa mothered her, but her main goal would always be the care and satisfaction of her adored Byron.

Teresa's father, Count Gamba, heard of their lack of discretion and was appalled. They were able to delay parting for awhile when

Byron made a second large loan to her husband, who ignored Count Gamba's objections to the arrangement. Finally, though, under pressure from his father-in-law, Count Guiccioli ordered Teresa to return. He wrote out a set of strict rules. Fearing public disgrace for the Gamba family and its five unmarried daughters, Byron persuaded Teresa to agree to her husband's demands.

Byron toyed again with the idea of returning to England with Allegra, but when he wrote his farewell to Teresa, she pitched a scene that finally defeated her elderly husband. He asked Byron to return to Ravenna for Christmas. Byron moved into the second floor of the count's palazzo with Allegra and his menagerie, which included a crane, a badger, dogs, and monkeys.

By April the count lost patience with the lovers' indiscreet displays of affection. Supported by her family, Teresa petitioned the Pope for a deed of separation. After the Pope granted her petition, Teresa went back to her own family. Byron stayed on alone at Guiccioli's palace for a time. He moved Allegra to a villa close to Teresa's father's home and visited both daughter and mistress from time to time. Byron committed himself to Teresa. Although they could not marry, he became almost a member of the Gamba family.

They were proud aristocrats. Both Count Gamba and his son Pietro belonged to a revolutionary organization, the Carbonari, bent on overthrowing the Italian aristocracy and the hated Austrian rule. Byron's sympathies and soon his actions joined with the Carbonari. The police kept him and the Gambas under close surveillance. Revolutionary friends placed him in real danger when they stored arms in his home.

On July 18, Pietro and his father were banished from Ravenna because of their political views. On December 9, 1820, a commandant of troops was shot outside Byron's door. Byron had him carried inside and the man died in an upstairs room of Byron's villa. Perhaps because of this act of compassion, he was not ordered to leave with the Gambas. When Teresa's husband demanded she return to him or enter a convent, she fled to join her father, the Gamba family settling in Pisa.

In the turbulence of 1821, Byron began the metaphysical dramatic poem, *Cain*. In it he concluded that even the gods are not happy. A sort of stoic self-reliance is the only answer to the hopelessness of human dreams.

Because of the increasingly violent nature of life in Italy, Byron decided Allegra needed to be in a safe place. He sent her to the convent at Bagnacavallo. This disturbed Claire, who had not anticipated Allegra's living away from Byron or receiving a Catholic education. Byron ignored Claire's concerns and the warnings expressed by others that the unheated, strictly run convent was situated in a marshy area that could cause health problems. He sent Allegra there on March 1, 1821.

Byron followed Teresa to Pisa. They became part of a group of expatriate English intellectuals that included the Shelleys along with Leigh and Marianne Hunt and their six uncontrolled, dishevelled children. Byron supported the Hunts, as Leigh was to work with him on a new journal, *The Liberal*. Byron would contribute works such as his "Vision of Judgment," a scathing poem in which the recently deceased King George III seeks admission into heaven.

Byron had chosen not to visit Allegra before he moved to Pisa, although she wrote, begging him to come. After Shelley went to see the little girl, he tried to persuade Byron to take Allegra back into his home, arguing that the convent was not well constructed. Byron seemed to agree, but then went on without her.

Claire, having heard rumors of the convent's being cold with poor food, wrote to Byron begging him to remove their daughter, or at least let Claire visit her. He refused. Claire traveled to Pisa with desperate plans to convince the Shelleys to help her abduct Allegra, but they urged caution.

Claire's worst fears came true when Allegra came down with a fever in mid-April. Reports came to Byron of Allegra's illness, bleedings by doctors, and finally of her death on April 20, 1822. Teresa handled all arrangements for the grief-stricken Byron. They shipped Allegra's body to England for burial outside the church at Harrow.

Allegra's tragedy was only the first blow. On July 13, 1822, a desperate Mary Shelley arrived at Byron's home with her friend Jane Williams, asking if had heard from Shelley. Their husbands had gone to Leghorn, where Shelley signed a will and then set sail for home in his boat, the *Don Juan*. A storm blew up and the sailors vanished. A few days later, Shelley's body washed ashore as William's had already done. Edward John Trelawny, a soldier of fortune and member of the

English circle at Pisa, identified the body. He oversaw its being covered in lime and buried on the beach.

On August 16, Byron and Hunt joined Trelawny to uncover and cremate Shelley's remains there on the sand. As the flames rose, they threw salt, sugar, incense, and wine on the body. Byron swam in the sea during part of the hours it took for his friend's body to become ashes. Byron later wrote to Moore, "All of Shelley was consumed, except his *heart*, which would not take the flame, and is now preserved in spirits of wine." (Marchand, 1025)

Byron intervened for the heart to be given to Mary. He also served as executor of Shelley's will and refused the bequest his friend had left for him. However, that night, following the cremation, after the remains were sealed in a box, the men drank heavily, turning in relief to silly songs and jokes. The next day, a seriously sunburned Byron was sick.

No matter the tragic events that occurred, and in spite of Teresa's attempts to sometimes censor or try to direct *Don Juan* to make it more romantic, Byron continued to write. His work has been criticized as uneven, but Byron turned his exile to triumph with lines written and rewritten during tumultuous times. He composed *Don Juan* through revolution, romance, relocations, and deaths of loved ones. Although never finished, it would become his masterpiece.

WAR AND DEATH

Byron's life in Italy stagnated. He loved Teresa, but their settled, almost-married arrangement bored him. Thoughts of moving to South America with Allegra were dashed on the rocks of her death, and he missed Shelley. Byron longed for escape into action.

The poet turned to Greece. Greek revolutionaries had begun training troops to combat their Turkish oppressors. In England, a sympathetic Greek Committee that included Hobhouse formed to support the rebels. Although skeptical that the Greek patriots could achieve independence, Byron admired their courage. A sense of purpose roused in him. He joined the Greek Committee with plans to go to Greece to work for the cause. He committed himself and his fortune. Far from having money problems, through the sale of

Newstead, more care in spending, inheritances, and his writing, he had made that fortune considerable. By the time he went to Greece his income equaled that of the United States' president.

But Teresa made his leaving an ordeal. Their bonds remained so strong he feared she would influence him not to leave for Greece in 1823, as she had decided not to sail for England in 1819. Teresa fought pressure from the Pope and her family to reconcile with her husband. She wanted to follow Byron to Greece but finally, tearfully, agreed to go to Ravenna with her father.

Byron knew he caused Teresa pain even though he assured her they would be together again someday. He wrote to his friend Lady Blessington, "There is something I am convinced in the poetical temperament that precludes happiness, not only to the person who has it, but to those connected with him." (Marchand, 1072)

Byron paid for the Hunts to go to Florence, glad to be rid of people who had sneered at his aristocratic manners while they accepted his money. He gave them his share of *The Liberal* along with rights to his works already published in it.

He included the adventure-loving Trelawny as his companion in the Greek project, along with Teresa's brother Pietro. Byron also employed a young doctor, Francesco Bruno, and long-time servants Fletcher and the Venetian Tita with six others, one a black man Byron hired away from Trelawny. In spite of Byron's superstitious nature, they boarded the chartered ship, *Hercules* on Friday, July 13, 1823. Byron, remembering the soothsayer's warning to his mother, believed that he was fated to die in his thirty-seventh year in any case.

Bad winds delayed them until July 16. When they had finally launched, they put in at Leghorn, where Byron happily received original verses mailed to him by Goethe and books sent by Augusta. On the ship, he played with his dogs, boxed, fenced, swam, and used pistols to target practice.

On August 1, they dropped anchor at the port of Argosti in Cephalonia, a British protectorate in the neutral Ionian Islands. Byron learned that his contact from the Greek Committee had left for England, leaving no instructions or information. As *Hercules* lingered, Byron, never certain of his reception from the English, was reassured by a warm welcome from Colonel Napier, the British resident. The regiment there even hosted him in their mess, drinking his health before dinner.

The Greeks were overjoyed to see him, knowing he was wealthy and internationally famous. Byron responded most warmly to the Suliotes, southern Albanian warriors who were now refugees in the Ionian Islands. They reminded Byron of his earlier travels in the East. He hired forty of them to be his bodyguards. It was a mistake. They were greedy, undisciplined mercenaries. Trelawny wrote,"[d]ay and night they clung to his heels like a pack of jackals, till he stood at bay like a hunted lion...." (Marchand, 1103)

He waited weeks for the Greek Committee or the Greek provisional government to advise what he should do next. He did find some pleasant ways to pass the time. He debated religious doctrine with the English garrison's physician, Dr. James Kennedy, who did his best to convert the poet. Byron impressed Kennedy and others sitting in on their discussions with his knowledge of the Bible and of religious commentaries.

He and his companions also made a sightseeing trip to Ithaca, scene of adventures of the ancient hero, Ulysses. It was not an easy tour. Byron struggled with sickness and mood swings.

During the trip he met a family whose fifteen-year-old son, Loukas, was away fighting, but soon joined them. He became Byron's pageboy. Byron loved Loukas as he had Edleston. Loukas did not return the passion, although he stayed with Byron. Byron's last love would never be requited.

The Greeks had split into factions, each seeking Byron's power and influence. Not sure how to proceed, Byron took a house in nearby Metaxata to wait for events to sort themselves out. Trelawny, frustrated by Byron's hesitance, went on to Missolonghi on the mainland.

The Committee in London finally urged Byron to handle a loan to the Greek government. Although the situation frustrated the man, who had seen his trip to Greece as a sort of heroic privilege, he wrote to Hobhouse, "If Greece should fall, I will bury myself in the ruins. If she should establish her independence, I will take up my residence in some part or other—perhaps Attica." (Untermeyer, 413)

Finally, in November, Byron prepared to go to the mainland. He would contribute money, arms, horses, and his own organizational skills to the Greeks. He launched his small, fast mistico at last on December 30, with Pietro in a companion boat carrying cargo. From Missolonghi, Col. Leicester Stanhope of the Greek Committee wrote, "All are looking forward to Lord Byron's arrival as they would to the coming of a Messiah." (Marchand, 1147)

At two in the morning, while they were still at sea, a Turkish ship loomed ahead. The mistico's captain ordered absolute silence, and they escaped into the darkness. At dawn, sighting another Turkish vessel between them and the port at Missolonghi, the mistico veered into a creek, where Loukas and others disembarked to be safer and seek help. Pursued by the Turks, Byron's boat slipped from creek to creek until finally reaching safety in the harbor of Dragomestre.

When Byron proceeded from the boat in his red uniform, he was greeted by gun salutes and cheering crowds. He had seen Missolonghi in 1809, so he knew what to expect. According to Marchand, the fishing village consisted of "dingy houses clustered on the flat, unwholesome promontory which stretched from the marshes of the mainland into the shallow lagoon." (Marchand, 1155) Sand spits and mud dunes separated the lagoon from the gulf. Varassova Mountain rose 3,000 feet out of the water at one end. Byron's three-story house stood at the edge of the promontory. At high tide or during rainy days it could only be reached by boat.

Troops and equipment filled the ground floor, with the first floor occupied by officers, including Stanhope and a printing press he used to publish news to the Greek people. Byron and his servants lived in the sparsely furnished second floor. When the ground behind the house dried enough, Byron trained troops there. He and Stanhope set up a press and dispensary. Once, Byron sheltered a Turkish prisoner in his home. When sailors broke in demanding the Turk, Byron forced them out at gunpoint.

He had to deal with conflicts between his barbaric Suliotes, now 500 in number, other German and Swedish mercenaries, and the townspeople. There were also skirmishes between Turkish and Greek ships on the gulf near his house. Through it all, Byron kept his commitment to Greek freedom. He put himself on the simple rations of his troops and lived austerely in the cold, damp climate.

Byron had matured, become the man of action, and by that means achieved a kind of greatness. But on the night before his thirty-sixth birthday, he gave way to friends' urging that he return to writing. Perhaps thinking of Loukas, he composed the plaintive "On This Day I Complete My Thirty-Sixth Year."

He welcomed the arrival of William Parry, a firemaster and mechanic bringing cannon sent from London by the Greek Committee. By now virtually the commander-in-chief in Missolonghi, Byron began to train troops for an assault on Lepanto, held by the Turks. However, the Suliotes became so unreasonable and untrustworthy that Byron finally lost his patience and fired them on February 15. Later that day they agreed to reform and he took them back, but the attack on Lepanto had to be postponed.

That evening, he called for cider while chatting with Stanhope and Parry. After drinking it, he stood up and stumbled, his mouth pulled to one side. Parry caught Byron as the poet went into a seizure-like convulsion. He came out of it in moments, asking, "Is not this Sunday?" When told it was, he responded, "I should have thought it most strange if it were not." (Maurois, 525) Byron believed Sundays were unlucky for him.

At noon the next day, Byron reluctantly gave in to Dr. Bruno's insistence that he be bled. Bruno applied leeches too close to Byron's temporal artery, causing a hemorrhage. Fletcher ran to the dispensary for Dr. Julius Millingen, a German in the Greek government service. Millingen succeeded in the excruciating process of cauterizing the vein. Byron muttered, "In this world there is nothing but pain." (Maurois, 526) His bleeding stopped sometime after 11:00 p.m.

In the days that followed, Byron, weak and suffering now from eye inflammations, worked from his rooms. Keeping order among his Suliotes demanded constant effort. He strove to establish humane treatment for prisoners on both sides. He showed concern for Turkish widows and orphans as well, even making plans to adopt one little Turkish girl and send her to Teresa, although in the end she went to the Kennedys at Byron's expense. He sent many Turkish women and children to Prevesa and its English consul for protection.

Late February 1824 found Byron physically and mentally depleted. He worried that he would have another seizure. He called himself "a young old man." (Marchand, 1187) He considered leaving Greece and brooded over his past. A letter from Augusta with a miniature portrait of Ada and a description of her daily life by Annabella brightened his gloom.

But troubles continued when a Suliote murdered a Swedish officer and frightened English mechanics asked to be sent home.

Byron paid the Suliotes to leave Missolonghi. Just after their exit an earthquake hit. Ironically, as progress in Missolonghi floundered, Byron heard that he was now a hero in England.

He kept a guard of fifty-six men and marched with them, or rode when weather permitted. However, his household was disintegrating into chaos. In March, the weather turned worse, and Byron suffered dizzy spells, anxiety attacks, and mood swings. He still labored to bring unity to the Greek factions, holding out the promise of loans they needed badly. The leaders of the two main factions and Byron scheduled a meeting at Salona. If reconciliation succeeded, many believed Byron would be offered the title of Governor-General of Greece. But torrential rains stranded him in Missolonghi. He told Parry, "My situation here is unbearable." (Marchand, 1205)

On April 9, Byron and Pietro were caught in pelting rain while riding. They returned across the lagoon by boat. Two hours later, Byron felt chills, ached, and turned feverish. The next day he sent for Parry to discuss best uses for a large English loan. He planned to subsidize the summer campaign himself, funding artillery and boats. Later, he grew worse and sent for Bruno. Bruno and Millingen argued for bleeding in spite of Byron's objection that "[t]here are many more die of the lancet than the lance." (Maurois, 532)

A hurricane struck, preventing Byron from leaving by boat for better medical treatment in Zante. In the days that followed he took hot baths and dosed with castor oil, antimony powder, henbane, broth, and arrowroot. He grew worse. He spoke with Parry of religion, seeming resigned and not afraid to die. The physicians pressured him constantly to submit to more bleeding.

The doctors finally persuaded him to be bled by suggesting that he might go insane if he refused. Bruno and Millingen drew a pound of blood. Two hours later they took another. Three hours later they asked to do it again, but Byron refused. Next day, however, they bled him twice. He became alternately incoherent and able to speak calmly.

By Easter Sunday, Byron lay near death. Townspeople moved quietly, not wanting to disturb him. When awake, Byron read letters and spoke briefly to friends. Bruno, Millingen, and two other doctors applied twelve leeches to Byron's temples and removed two pounds of blood. He bitterly told Fletcher, "The doctors have assassinated me...." (Marchand, 1226–1227)

Later, Byron tried to state his last wishes, but Fletcher could only understand broken phrases, including "my wife—my child—Ada—my poor sister...." (Marchand, 1228)

At 6:00 p.m. on April 18, Byron said his last words, "I want to sleep now." (Marchand, 1228) He lost consciousness, and the doctors bled him all night. He died on April 19, 1824, at twilight. Almost simultaneously a violent thunderstorm struck Missolonghi. The Greeks, who believed the deaths of heroes are announced by signs, saw the lightening and knew Byron was dead.

At dawn the next day, thirty-seven guns fired—one for each year of Byron's life. The doctors performed an autopsy and discovered Byron had suffered from an inflamed brain. They described it as like an old man's.

His funeral took place in Missolonghi, but other towns and cities in Greece held memorial services as well. Byron's remains, with the exception of some parts kept for burial in Greece, were shipped back to England. The funeral cortege in London included many fine carriages, mostly empty, as his fellow aristocrats wanted to acknowledge him, but not enough to be seen in person at the notorious man's funeral. He was buried at the family vault at Hucknall in Nottinghamshire.

Another drama took place in England among Byron's surviving friends and relatives. Thomas Moore had possession of Byron's memoirs. At Augusta's pleading, Moore reluctantly gave in and agreed to the burning of the original and its only copy.

Byron's dramatic and self-dramatized life ended. His humor and vibrant, unblinking insights into human experience had influenced war-weary Europeans. He had challenged conservative thinking that followed the Napoleonic era. The literary youth of England especially mourned his passing.

Readers continue to discover in Byron the great pain and rich joys of a life lived intensely, in courageous exploration of the both the follies and the glories at the core of human nature.

Works Cited

Drinkwater, John. *The Pilgrim of Eternity: Byron—A Conflict*. New York: George H. Doran, 1925.

Highet, Gilbert. "The Poet and His Vulture." *Byron: A Collection of Critical Essays*, Ed. Paul West. Englewood Cliffs, N.J.: Prentice-Hall, 1963.

Jack, Ian. *English Literature 1815–1832*. Oxford: Clarendon Press, 1964.

Marchand, Leslie. *Byron: A Biography*. New York: Knopf, 1957.

Maurois, Andre. *Byron*. Trans. Hamish Miles, New York: D. Appleton-Century Co., 1937.

McGann, Jerome J., ed. *Byron*. Oxford: Oxford University Press, 1986.

Praz, Mario. "Metamorphoses of Satan." *Byron. A Collection of Critical Essays*. Ed. Paul West. Englewood Cliffs, N.J.: Prentice-Hall, 1963.

Strickland, Margot. *The Byron Women*. New York: St. Martin's Press, 1974.

Untermeyer, Louis. *Lives of the Poets: The Story of One Thousand Years of English and American Poetry*. New York: Simon and Schuster, 1959.

Wain, John. "The Search for Identity." *Byron: A Collection of Critical Essays*. Ed. Paul West. Englewood Cliffs, N.J.: Prentice-Hall, 1963.

DUKE PESTA

"Darkness Visible":
Byron and the Romantic Anti-Hero

The life of the historical George Gordon, Lord Byron (1788–1824) is obscured by light and illuminated by darkness.[1] Like Satan, the larger than life anti-hero of Milton's *Paradise Lost*, the real Byron is a mass of contradictions, a figure more elusive and harder to trace the more history focuses on him. It will be remembered that Milton's Satan reinvented himself in the lightless regions of hell and cursed the sun that exposed the cracks and flaws in his countenance. So, too, Byron's legend was crafted in the shadows of rumor, innuendo, self-exile, and misdeed. Indeed, it would be Byron who unwittingly described his own paradoxical nature, "all that's best of dark and bright," in "She Walks in Beauty," the poem most recognized as Byronic by modern readers.

Dark and brilliant, melancholy and vivacious, overtly sexual and sexually ambiguous, the shadowy side of the Byron persona has attained the stature of such dangerously attractive figures as Casanova, the Marquis de Sade, and Rasputin. On the other hand, his artistic achievements, panache, and free spirit call to mind the heroic and romantic exploits of the likes of the Scarlet Pimpernel, Cyrano de Bergerac, and Lawrence of Arabia. His poetry may have brought him fame and prominence, but it was his life—the way he lived and the way he allowed people to think he lived—that secured his place as one of the most imitated and misunderstood personalities ever to appear on the world stage. At once a poet, cavalier, athlete, soldier, activist, critic, notorious rake, and fashion-setter, Byron cut a dashing figure despite being relatively short and hampered by a club foot that caused him to limp all his life. He had trouble controlling his weight, especially as he aged, but this in no way seemed to diminish his amorous appeal.

Byron was famous for his affairs (rumored and real) with numerous women and periodically with young men. At a very early age, he developed a hopeless infatuation with his neighbor and cousin, Mary Chaworth, and the gossip surrounding his apparent affair with his half-sister Augusta Leigh in 1813 both scandalized and titillated English society. Upon seeing Byron for the first time, Lady Caroline Lamb, who would also become his lover, wrote in her journal the famous observation that he was "mad, bad, and dangerous to know." Even his early and tragic death in 1824 at age 36, which did much to repair his reputation back home in England, was not without scandal and spectacle. Byron would never again see England after fleeing in disgrace in 1816. When his corpse, worn by the ravages of time, marred by a slipshod autopsy, and bearing the marks of ill-living, disease, and death, was finally seen back in England, many of his most intimate acquaintances either did not recognize the man or doubted the body was his. Augusta Leigh, who knew Byron's body as a brother and a lover, and who bore his child, remarked that in death the figure was so changed "that I could scarcely persuade myself it was he—not a vestige of what he was." And, upon viewing the corpse, Byron's friend and traveling companion John Cam Hobhouse observed:

> The face of the corpse did not bear the slightest resemblance to my dear friend—the mouth was distorted & half open showing those teeth in which poor fellow he once so prided himself quite discoloured by the spirits—his upper lip was shaded with mustachios which gave a totally new character to his face—his cheeks were long and bagged over the jaw—his nose was quite prominent at the bridge and sank in between the eyes—his eye brows shaggy & lowering—his skin like dull parchment. It did not seem to be Byron.[2]

Death, of course, is a notorious disfigurer that obscures what we were in life, making our bodies, and often our accomplishments, finally unrecognizable. But in Byron's case, death merely continued a process that was begun by the poet himself and that continues unabated to this day in the mysterious and ever-evolving figure of the Byronic Hero.

The dramatic circumstances of Byron's life are inseparable from the Byronic myth, and an understanding of both is essential to any appreciation of Byron's poetry of light and darkness. Byron was conceived in France in 1787, where his parents, Captain John "Mad Jack" Byron and Catherine Gordon Byron, had moved to avoid their creditors. His mother, insisting that her child be born in England, left her husband in France, where he died in 1791, possibly by suicide. Byron was born January 22, 1788, into a family with noble roots and alarmingly poor finances. When his great-uncle the fifth Lord Byron died in 1798, the precocious and melancholy ten-year-old inherited the family title and the dilapidated Newstead Abbey in Nottinghamshire. As a child, Byron was sensitive and acutely aware of the handicap caused by his club foot. To compensate for this infirmity, Byron learned how to fence and fight; he also became a remarkably strong swimmer. (When Byron visited Greece as a young man, he passed the time by swimming the Hellespont, a distance of some three miles, recreating the heroic exploit of Leander, who was reputed to have swum the distance to visit his estranged love Hero.) After being introduced to sex by a drunken nurse named May Gray, the young Byron was sent to boarding school. After boarding school, Byron enrolled at Trinity College, Cambridge in 1805, where he quickly amassed enormous debts with his reckless spending and lavish lifestyle (among other things, he kept a tame bear in his room) and raised eyebrows by exploring bisexual relationships.

As was the custom for dissipated nobility at the time, Byron neglected his studies, but he did write verses, including the volume *Fugitive Pieces*, published without Byron's name in 1806. Byron presented a first copy to the Reverend J. T. Becher of Southwell, who took offense at one poem in particular, the sexually charged "To Mary," which Becher insisted was "too warmly drawn." The abashed Byron reacted to this criticism by rounding up and destroying as many of the volumes as he could locate. His success in disposing of them can be seen in the fact that only four copies exist today, among them the Reverend Becher's own copy. In "To Mary," Byron chronicles his bittersweet recollections of a recently ended love affair. Even at an early age, Byron's poetic style is concerned with shades of dark and light. Like Milton's Satan, and John Donne before him, Byron chastises the sun, that "glaring God of Day," who divulges the sexual acts that passed between the lovers "regardless of his *peeping* ray." It was not Byron's sun that Becher found too warm; rather, it was the deeds done in darkness between Mary and her lover that generated heat:

> [I] smile to think how oft we've done,
> What prudes declare a sin to act is,
> And never but in darkness practice,
> Fearing to trust the tell tale sun.[3] (II. 37–40)

Warmth without light, heat without sun, and a burning passion that is self-consuming in its intensity—these are the incipient hallmarks of the Byronic Hero: "Though love than ours could ne'er be truer, / Yet flames too fierce themselves destroy." Throughout his adult life and in his numerous relationships, Byron never seemed able to sustain the intensity of his initial passions long, quickly tiring of his many lovers. This restless itch to rove, this unquenchable thirst to drink in the new and the strange, would also become a key component of the Byronic Hero, and the legacy can be seen in such literary descendants as Heathcliffe in *Wuthering Heights* and Rochester in *Jane Eyre*, and such cinematic descendants as James Dean and Marlon Brando.

In 1807, Byron published another volume of poems, *Hours of Idleness*, which received a scathing notice from the *Edinburgh Review* in 1808. A depressed Byron responded in 1809 with the spirited and successful satire *English Bards and Scotch Reviewers*. In the same year, his twenty-first, Byron took his seat in the House of Lords and embarked on a grand tour of Portugal, Spain, Albania, Greece and Turkey in the company of his friend Hobhouse. It was on this trip that Byron began to write the semi-autobiographical *Childe Harold's Pilgrimage*, a poetic journal that would take eight years to compose. The first two cantos, which would not be published until 1812, loosely chronicle the first year of his travels, recounting the story of a rebellious outsider who seeks new experiences and distractions after a life spent indulging in all manner of sin and sexual license.

Immediately upon publication, *Childe Harold* secured lasting fame for Byron and guaranteed his position as the first poet/celebrity of the modern era. Looking back on the event, Byron would remark, "I woke up one morning and found myself famous." The graphic sensuality and suggestive detail of the poem, combined with the scandal of self-revelation, quickly made Byron the talk of London. From the very opening stanzas, the diary-like quality of Byron's poem, together with his frank and intimate verses, expose a life at once bright with promise and dogged by shadow. We find a hero who "bask'd him in the noon-tide sun, / Disporting there like any other fly" (I. 4. 1–2); he was, like Byron, a gifted youth

> Who ne in virtue's ways did take delight;
> But spent his days in riot most uncouth,
> And vex'd with mirth the drowsy ear of Night.
> Ah, me! in sooth he was a shameless wight,
> Sore given to revel and ungodly glee;
> Few earthly things found favour in his sight
> Save concubines and carnal companie,
> And flaunting wassailers of high and low degree. (I. 2–9)

The far-off locales and exotic exploits of Harold resonated deeply with English readers seeking an escape from the regimen and orderliness of the Enlightenment. Harold's decision to leave England and seek adventure and danger in far-off lands appealed to both the wanderlust of the pampered social elite and the imaginative fancy of the duty-bound middle class. Like them, Harold "felt the fullness of satiety: / Then loath'd he in his native land to dwell, / Which seem'd to him more lone than Eremite's sad cell." (I. 4. 7–9).

In a tellingly wry letter written to Thomas Moore in 1817, Byron responds to Moore's praise of *Childe Harold's Pilgrimage*:

> I am glad you like it; it is a fine indistinct piece of poetical desolation, and my favourite. I was half mad during the time of its composition, between metaphysics, mountains, lakes, love unextinguishable, thoughts unutterable, and the nightmare of my own delinquencies. I should, many a good day, have blown my brains out, but for the recollection that it would have given pleasure to my mother-in-law.[4]

This carefully cultivated "devil-may-care attitude" toward his poem is part an acknowledgement of his own nobility (for the aristocracy, writing verse was an avocation, not a legitimate calling) and part a studied disavowal of Harold's libertinism, a disavowal understood to actually deepen the association. In this, Byron was unlike his fellow Romantics, Shelley and Keats in particular, for whom the call to poetry was a sublime destiny that could not be ignored. Byron did not overtly share Shelley's belief that poetry could alter the course of the world, nor did Byron rally to Shelley's conviction that he should use his talents solely for the purpose of enlightening mankind.[5] From the moment *Childe Harold* appeared on the literary scene, it would no longer be possible to distinguish between Byron the man and Byron the Romantic Hero. As he insisted in an assertion characteristic of our notion of the Byronic Hero, "The only pleasure of fame is that it paves the way to pleasure."[6]

But the Byronic Hero was more than just a transgressive lothario seeking new and ever more dissipated diversions. This was merely the dark side of the persona, those aspects of the legend that underscored his danger, sexual potency, and disregard for the conventions of "decent" society. The Byronic Hero was also fiercely proud in his assertion of individual human dignity, a glorious exemplum of personal freedom and violent self-expression. In this he manages at one and the same time to anticipate both Thoreau and Nietzsche. As the Industrial Revolution progressed and cities began to overflow with refugees from rural farms and villages, the Byronic notion of space and the freedom to travel to vast, exotic lands became synonymous with greatness of soul and independence of thought. When Byron took up the tale of Harold in Canto III in 1816, he had left England for the last time in the wake of scandal and sensation and had settled in Italy. The moving description of Harold at the opening of Canto III is all the more stirring and poignant because of the obvious autobiographical associations:

> But soon he knew himself the most unfit
> Of men to herd with Man; with whom he held
> Little in common; untaught to submit
> His thoughts to others, though his soul was quell'd
> In youth by his own thoughts; still uncompell'd,
> He would not yield dominion of his mind

To spirits against whom his own rebell'd;
Proud though in desolation, which could find
  A life within himself, to breathe without mankind. (III. 12)

The description is almost Miltonic, and the image of the great apostate, censured and banished, but not demeaned in spirit, is the source of the attraction and the repulsion that he inspires in others. Set apart in splendid isolation and misunderstood by a world beneath him, the Byronic loner communes only with his own capacious spirit, embodying a melancholy and a dignity beyond the grasp of ordinary men.

After the publication of Cantos I and II of *Childe Harold's Pilgrimage* in 1812, Byron's life and celebrity exploded. Within three days of publication, all 500 first-edition copies had been sold. Before it was even published, Samuel Rogers showed a copy of the poem to Lady Caroline Lamb, who was involved in a passionless marriage with the politician William Lamb. Desperate for excitement and intrigue, Lady Caroline was instantly drawn to the figure of Harold, and when it was revealed that the character was drawn from the life of the author, she resolved to meet Byron at any cost. When Rogers informed her of Byron's club foot, she remarked, "If he is as ugly as Aesop, I must see him"; once she saw him, she observed, "that beautiful, pale face is my fate." In March they began a torrid affair, which, for Byron, had reached its peak by May. Byron's growing aloofness sent Lady Caroline into hysterics, and she dressed as a page to gain access to his chambers, where, after great consternation, Byron and Hobhouse persuade her to return to her home. The love-struck Caroline even went so far as to mail Byron her pubic hair, but to no avail. In the meantime, Byron had fallen in love with and proposed to Annabella Milbanke, the cousin of Lady Caroline's husband William Lamb, but in October 1812 Anabella rejected his proposal and questioned his character.

The personal maelstrom that threatened to engulf Byron intensified in 1813, as he found himself romantically linked to Lady Oxford, continued to dodge the advances of the desperate Lady Caroline, resumed his correspondence with Anna Milbanke, and, most ominously, began his incestuous affair with his half-sister Augusta Leigh. In January 1814, Byron finished writing *The Corsair*, perhaps the most famous example of "orientalist" poetry produced during the Romantic period. In this work Byron further capitalizes on the public's demand for exotic tales of adventure and romance set in dreamy, eastern locales. *The Corsair* was wildly successful, selling 10,000 copies on the first day of its publication and over 25,000 copies in the first month. No doubt brisk sales were enhanced by the obvious parallels between the author and Conrad, the aristocratic, idealistic, and disenchanted hero of the poem. Conrad is the typical Byronic outcast, brooding, potent, and dismissive of social convention. An aristocrat by birth, Conrad flees the confines of traditional society and becomes the leader of a band of pirates, or "corsairs," whose prime objective is the disruption of Turkish shipping in open defiance of the cruel and autocratic Turkish Pasha.

The interplay between light and dark, artistically, morally, and even racially, is also a key component of orientalist poetry, and this no doubt attracted Byron, whose own poetry depended entirely on such juxtapositions. Thus, Byron benefited aesthetically from this trend toward the exotic and the oriental, even as he in large part created the genre by intermingling the lights and shades of his own frenetic experience. And, as can be seen in Byron's poetic description of Conrad, the points of demarcation between Byron and the Byronic Hero continued to blur:

> Sun-burnt his cheek, his forehead high and pale
> The sable curls in wild profusion veil;
> And oft perforce his rising lip reveals
> The haughtier thought it curbs, but scarce conceals.
> [...]
> There was a laughing Devil in his sneer,
> That raised emotions both of rage and fear;
> And where his frown of hatred darkly fell,
> Hope withering fled—and Mercy sighed farewell!
>   (I. 9. 203–06; 223–26)

Here the pale, delicate features of the western aristocrat so praised by Lady Caroline have been darkened, toughened by a life of action amid sun and wind and sea. The "native son" has assimilated with his swarthy compatriots, racially, politically, and socially. The Byronic outsider has not just been accepted by the cultural "Other," he has become their leader. In this imaginative vision, at once colonizing and post-colonial, Byron's Conrad foreshadows such mysterious figures as Kurtz in Joseph Conrad's *Heart of Darkness*, and even the Tarzan legend.

Conrad's scornful sneer reveals his titanic disdain, that "laughing devil" that mocks, even as it rises above, the petty criticisms of a stagnant society. And the devilish and darkling frown that banishes hope and mercy again brings to mind Milton's Satan in his great address upon seeing the sun for the first time since his fall:

> O thou that with surpassing Glory crown'd,
> Look'st from thy sole Dominion like the God
> Of this new World; at whose sight all the Starrs
> Hide their diminisht heads; to thee I call,
> But with no friendly voice, and add thy name
> O Sun, to tell thee how I hate thy beams
> That bring to my remembrance from what state
> I fell, how glorious once above thy Spheare. (IV. 32–39)[7]

Satan's terrible fall and subsequent transformation from "Lucifer," the great bearer of light, to "Satan," the prince of darkness, was precipitated by his haughty pride and by his perverse ability to invert the very principles of light and darkness. This willful reshaping of reality is nowhere more apparent than in Satan's continual and protean self-fashioning. As we have seen, this audacious ability to remake the self and reshape reality, this sublime combination of pride and perversity, also defines the life and career of Byron, whose poetic works are dominated by corresponding images of light and darkness.

In a prefatory letter to the *The Corsair*, again addressed to Thomas Moore, Byron comments on the intermingling of his life and art, and on his unwillingness to shed light on the darkness of the association:

> With regard to my story, and stories in general, I should have been glad to have rendered my personages more perfect and amiable, if possible, inasmuch as I have been sometimes criticised, and considered no less responsible for their deeds and qualities than if all had been personal. Be it so—if I have deviated into the gloomy vanity of

"drawing from self," the pictures are probably like, since they are unfavourable; and if not, those who know me are undeceived, and those who do not, I have little interest in undeceiving. I have no particular desire that any but my acquaintance should think the author better than the beings of his imagination....[8]

Byron acknowledges both his sensitivity to the criticism directed at his personal life (by way of his artistic creations) and his disregard for such censure. The contradictory impulses of heightened sensitivity and a corresponding disdain that seems to "protest too much" explain some of the attractiveness of the Byronic Hero, providing a glimpse of the vulnerability that lies beneath the hardened exterior. There can be no melancholy without sensitivity, and the strident individuality of the Byronic Hero masks a profound loneliness and isolation. It is this spark of vulnerability, this glimpse of light at the core of the dark persona of the Byronic Hero, that so intrigues. This is as true in the life of Byron as in his poetic creations. Or, as Byron relates in verses that reveal Conrad's mind and his own:

There is no darkness like the cloud of mind,
On Grief's vain eye—the blindest of the blind!
Which may not—dare not see—but turns aside
To blackest shade—nor will endure a guide!
        (II. 22.685–661)

As Byron's fame and reputation increased with the publication of *The Corsair*, so too did the rumors and scandals that, in part, drove that fame. In April of 1814, Augusta Leigh gave birth to a daughter, Medora, who was widely thought to be Byron's child and who was named for the famous heroine of *The Corsair*. Perhaps in part to offset criticism of his conduct with Augusta Leigh, Byron again proposed to Annabella Milbanke (although this proposal would come in the mail, an ominous indication of future trouble), and this time she accepted.

From the very first moment of their engagement, Byron wavered about his decision, and it is remarkable that the wedding came off at all. Hobhouse remarked that "never was a bridegroom less in haste." On his way to Seaham Hall in Durham for the wedding,

Byron stopped to see Augusta at Six Mile Bottom, where he wrote a letter calling off the wedding, but he was persuaded by Augusta not to send it. The day before the ceremony, Byron's best man, Hobhouse, tried to talk the vicar out of performing the ceremony, arguing that Byron was a monster of cruelty, but to no avail. Byron and Annabella finally wed on January 2, 1815, and the marriage was predictably a disaster from the outset, as Byron alternately treated his bride with condescension and cruelty. The more Byron felt constrained by his marriage to the bookish Annabella, who proved to be rather humorless for Byron's taste and unusually fond of mathematics (Byron called her his "Princess of Parallelograms"), the more outlandishly he acted out. Among other things, Byron is said to have forced his bride to perform certain sexual acts against her will (even while eight months pregnant). During the few calmer periods of their married life, Annabella could not appreciate or understand the humor behind Byron's little jokes, as when he tellingly referred to himself as the "avatar of a fallen angel." During the rougher patches, Byron would taunt Annabella by holding up to her the superior charms of his half-sister Augusta, who actually moved in with the struggling couple in an attempt to calm the troubled marital waters. Crushing debts and intense pressure from creditors compounded the problems in their relationship, causing Byron to alternate between bouts of heavy drinking and suicidal despair and to manifest his displeasure in increasingly violent expressions of temper. During one particularly heated argument, Byron fired his pistols at the ceiling.

Besides drinking, Byron also sought relief from his self-imposed marital hell by spending more and more time at the theater, where he could escape not only his wife but also his increasingly relentless creditors. Understandably, this was not the most prolific period of Byron's life, although there were some noteworthy accomplishments in 1815, including the publication in April of the *Hebrew Melodies*. These poems, most of which treat themes from Hebrew scripture, were written in conjunction with Issac Nathan's musical renditions of ancient Jewish melodies. Nathan first offered the job of writing the accompanying verses to Sir Walter Scott, and when he refused, Byron agreed to the collaboration. The *Melodies* were published by Nathan and John Braham (born John Abraham), the talented and popular tenor who had nothing to do with the musical arrangement or the composition of the verses, but did help advertise the work by singing the finished pieces. In embarking on this project, Nathan hoped to capitalize on the vogue for the exotic that Byron had helped to create. To satisfy this craving for unique experience, Romantic sensibilities did not just look east; they also looked backward, to great, fallen civilizations (witness Shelley's "Ozymandias") and strange and mystic cultures (witness Coleridge's "Kubla Khan" and "Christabel," poems that Byron greatly admired). Like the Gothic culture of the Middle Ages, the culture of the ancient Hebrews, at once so alien and so familiar, was a particularly attractive option, bringing together such disparate associations as the Kabbala and the Ten Commandments.

It was precisely this perceived interplay of dark and light in the culture of the ancient Hebrews that made Byron the perfect poet for this collaboration. Nathan's music perfectly complemented Byron's verses, conveying a sense of the sacred and the profane, the sublime and the secular, that characterizes all of Byron's poetry and that is also a hallmark of the Hebrew Scriptures. This impulse can be seen in the delicate *chiaroscuro* effects of "She Walks in Beauty": "One shade the more, one ray the less, / Had half impair'd the nameless grace," as well as in the stirring connection of music and melancholy in "My Soul is Dark":

> My soul is dark—Oh! quickly string
> The harp I yet can brook to hear;
> [...]
> But bid the strain be wild and deep,
> Nor let thy notes of joy be first:
> I tell thee, minstrel, I must weep,
> Or else this heavy heart will burst. (I. 1–2; II. 1–4)

Byron manages to evoke both the joy and the despair of the Psalms in this poem. And Byron understood, as did David before him, that the joy of praise and salvation could only be sung after great suffering and release. Both Byron and David felt the overwhelming call to express their deepest emotions in verse, and here we have the full force of the Romantic notion of "emotion recollected in tranquility," as Byron returns us back to the caves, to David's days of doubt and fear. Byron no doubt recollects his own dark days as well, experiences that forged in solitude the stark contrasts in his own personality, the strains "wild and deep" that evoke a darkness that sets in brilliant relief that brightness of the inner man. This quality of the Byronic Hero is perhaps best expressed in "Sun of the Sleepless":

> Sun of the sleepless! melancholy star!
> Whose tearful beam glows tremulously far,
> That show'st the darkness thou canst not dispel,
> How like art thou to joy remembered well!
> So gleams the past, the light of other days,
> Which shines, but warms not with its powerless rays;
> A night-beam Sorrow watcheth to behold,
> Distinct, but distant—clear—but, oh how cold!

Here, we return yet again to "darkness visible," to a powerless light that serves only to illustrate the darkness. Such, for Byron, are the joys of the past. Emotion recollected in tranquility may indeed be the stuff of poetry, but the vision, distinct and clear, brings no warmth.

1815 was not only a pivotal year for Byron, it was also a pivotal year for Europe, as the Continent witnessed the denouement of Napoleon's drama of world conquest. Byron had long been a great admirer of Napoleon and actually risked derision by keeping a bust of the emperor in his rooms during his boarding school days at Harrow. Byron could not fail to recognize in Napoleon many of the characteristics of the Byronic Hero, and there are a number of remarkable similarities between the two men. John Clubbe has observed:

> Both men could feel strong physical attraction for other men; both had a marked misogynistic streak. Both had sisters dearly beloved and a flawed first marriage. Both inspired exceptional loyalty among subordinates. Both were extremely superstitious ... Both read history by preference and liked to compare themselves with the great of the past, Napoleon with Alexander, Byron with figures from Diogenes to Rousseau, not forgetting the Emperor himself.[9]

Attempting to articulate the nature of his fascination with Napoleon shortly after he "abdicated the throne of the world," Byron wrote:

> I don't know—but I think *I*, even *I* (an insect compared with this creature), have set my life on casts not a millionth part of this man's.... Alas! this imperial diamond hath a flaw in it, and is now hardly fit to stick in a glazier's pencil.... But I won't give him up even now; though all his admirers have, 'like the thanes, fallen from him.'[10]

In his "Ode to Napoleon" (1814), Byron had written of the great man's fall, he who was "but yesterday a King! / And arm'd with Kings to strive," and who now is but "a nameless thing" (1–3), a poetic phrase that both recalls the fall of Priam in Virgil's *Aeneid* and anticipates Yeats' great reflection on age and obscurity in "Sailing to Byzantium." Here we have Byron's Romantic revision of the famous *ubi sunt* trope, that mournful and elegiac strain of "where have they gone" that also pervades Shelley's "Ozymandias." But Shelley's poem contains irony and censure, and the arrogant pronouncement found on the ruined statue of the mighty Ozymandias, "Look on my works ye mighty and despair," is met only with the silence of the sands.[11] There is something reproachful and moralistic here, subtly condemning the human vanity that made such pretension possible. Byron, too, is cognizant of the failure of great ambition; only for Byron and the Byronic Hero the emphasis falls as equally on the greatness of the effort as it does the irony of the fall. In the summer of 1815, Byron's own day of banishment was fast approaching, and he must have sensed something of his own situation in the meteoric rise and fall of Napoleon. This makes Byron's poem "Napoleon's Farewell" (1815) all the more poignant, highlighting as it does the blinding lights and impenetrable darks that comprise in equal measure the soul of the rebellious conqueror and the soul of poetic rebel. The eulogy is as much Byron's as Napoleon's:

> Farewell to the Land where the gloom of my Glory
> Arose and o'ershadowed the earth with her name—
> She abandons me now—but the page of her story,
> The brightest or blackest, is fill'd with my fame. (1–4)

The brightest and the blackest, or as Sir Philip Sidney once wrote, a combination framing "daintiest luster, mixed of shades and light."[12] But it was not justice or virtue that could bring down the Byronic Hero; those abstract and outdated conceptions merely marked the limitations of the conventional mind. Rather it was his own greatness of spirit, manifesting itself in ceaseless striving for an excellence defined on the individual's own terms, that guaranteed the outcast state of the Byronic Hero. In this regard, he recalled both Satan's apostasy and the nobly tragic figures of Adam and Eve as they made their exodus from Eden in *Paradise Lost*. He also foreshadowed the existential movement and the Nietzschean *Übermensch*.

By the end of 1815, Byron's behavior had become dangerously unpredictable and unstable. Even the calming influence of Augusta Leigh could not assuage his anger or mollify his dissatisfaction. As his debts mounted and his personal relationships deteriorated, Byron succumbed to his dark side, and his drinking and hostility increased to the point that Annabella believed him insane. On December 10, Annabella gave birth to a daughter, Augusta Ada; by January 15, 1816, Annabella had returned to the house of her parents, never to see Byron again. By March they had agreed to a legal separation. There is much speculation about the events surrounding the dissolution of the marriage. Byron seems to have been genuinely shocked and dismayed that things had taken such a turn and actually took steps to bring about a reconciliation. The fact that Byron ultimately agreed to the divorce with relatively little opposition has led some to conclude that Annabella threatened to reveal what she knew of Byron's incest and bisexuality. The fact that Annabella retained full custody of their child, which was certainly unusual at that time, seems to confirm the suspicion. Byron himself suspected that Annabella had broken into his desk and read his personal papers. It is true that Annabella kept careful record of Byron's excessive and shocking behavior during their marriage, and the rumors surrounding these documents did much to win her public sympathy.

It has been remarked that the only thing society celebrates more than an individual's meteoric rise to fame is his or her corresponding fall. Byron, who had been the romantic and literary lion of English society, had now become a pariah. Publicly disgraced, there was no charge leveled at him that was not credited in some quarter. Besides incest and sodomy, Byron stood accused of madness and sadism, and was supposed to possess an advanced case of syphilis. The periodicals battened on the scandal, producing parodies and outright attacks that cut Byron to the quick and made London unlivable. Byron could no longer attend the theater for fear of public reprisals, and many of his previous admirers turned on him with stinging condemnations.

On April 25, 1816, Byron left England for the last time, traveling through Belgium on his way to Switzerland. In a chivalrous and romantic gesture, Byron rode across the Continent in a carriage that was an exact replica of Napoleon's (which accounts for his avoiding France), stopping along the way to tour the Waterloo battlefield, the site where Byron's kindred spirit had seen his own hopes dashed. In Switzerland, Byron met Shelley for the first time and formed an immediate intellectual bond with him, spending the summer with Shelley's circle, a group that included Shelly's soon-to-be wife, Mary Godwin, and Claire Clairmont, Godwin's young stepdaughter, with whom Bryon had begun an affair while the two were still in England. From this association springs the following famous anecdote about Byron and the creation of Mary Shelley's *Frankenstein*. Inclement weather often forced the group indoors, where they took to reading ghost stories. On Byron's suggestion, the company each agreed to write an original ghost tale, which provided the opportunity for Mary Shelley to turn a terrifying dream into a classic novel of human darkness and transgression.

Something of Byron himself can be seen both in the obsession of Dr. Frankenstein and in the defiant isolation of his misunderstood creature. *Frankenstein*, too, is a work of transcendent light and primordial darkness, and even Shelley's subtitle for her novel, "The Modern Prometheus," captures something of the burgeoning Byron legend, calling to mind the terrible punishment inflicted on the mythological Prometheus for stealing fire from the gods in order to illuminate a savagely dark and ignorant world. In "Prometheus" (1816), his own poem on the theme, Byron understood only too well that the price to be paid for daring to evoke the light of the gods was the darkness of scorn and obloquy:

> Titan! to whose immortal eyes
> > The sufferings of mortality,

> Seen in their sad reality,
> Were not as things that gods despise;
> What was thy pity's recompense?
> A silent suffering, and intense;
> The rock, the vulture, and the chain,
> All that the proud can feel of pain ... (1–8)

Even worse than the physical suffering inflicted by the vulture that endlessly gnawed at his ever-regenerating liver, Prometheus had to endure the knowledge that his grand gesture could not be understood by those he hoped to illuminate. Byron repeatedly took solace for his own disgrace and self-imposed banishment by associating himself with those great figures from mythology and history—Satan, Cain, Prometheus, Icarus, Faustus, Napoleon—who themselves fell after flying too close to the sun.

Reinvigorated by his escape from London, Byron resumed the writing of *Childe Harold's Pilgrimage*, producing the acclaimed third canto by July. It was also during the summer of 1816 that Byron and Shelley sailed around Lake Geneva and toured the famous dungeons beneath the Chateau of Chillon. Here they viewed the cell where François de Bonnivard languished as a prisoner for four years in the sixteenth century (1532–1536). After seeing the path that Bonnivard had worn in the stones with his incessant pacing, Byron was so moved that he composed a sonnet in honor of the place, which was quickly transformed into *The Prisoner of Chillon*, his poetic account of Bonnivard's imprisonment. Bonnivard's prolonged and unjust isolation in the dark, dank cell beneath the gorgeous castle and lake touched a deeply responsive chord in Byron:

> There were no stars—no earth, no time—
> No check—no change—no good—no crime—
> But silence, and a stirless breath
> Which neither was of life nor death;
> A sea of stagnant idleness,
> Blind, boundless, mute, and motionless! (245–250)

For Byron and the Byronic Hero, physical and mental pain and suffering were not the worst torments to be endured. Even as

Prometheus was chained to the rock and subjected to excruciating physical pain, he could still assert his pride and dignity in the face of oppression by refusing to conform. As these verses from *The Prisoner of Chillon* reveal, the real terror was an enforced idleness, a revocation of all sensual experience, whereby one could be stripped of all external stimuli from which experience was derived. Only by looking inward and remaking experience could the Byronic Hero endure, as Byron's account of Bonnivard's eventual liberation makes clear:

> I learn'd to love despair.
> And thus when they appear'd at last,
> And all my bonds aside were cast,
> These heavy walls to me had grown
> A hermitage—and all my own! (374–378)

Once again, Byron's lines echo the willful defiance and self-reliance of Milton's Satan, who argued that "The mind is its own place, and in itself / Can make a Heav'n of Hell, a Hell of Heav'n" (I. 254–255).

In September 1816, Byron and Hobhouse set off for Italy. Along the way Byron was so deeply taken with the breathtaking scenery that he kept an "Alpine Journal" to record the spectacle for Augusta Leigh. Against this ancient and still pristine backdrop, Byron penned his poetic drama *Manfred*, a brooding reflection on the darker aspects of the Romantic spirit, written in the tradition of Marlowe's *Doctor Faustus* and Goethe's *Faust*. The play is set in the Alps, where Manfred, the play's overtly Byronic anti-hero, conjures up spirits as a way of escaping the torments imposed on his conscience by some terrible, unnamed transgression of his past. Many critics have assumed this crime had autobiographical associations, most likely incest between Manfred and his sister Astarte, which recalled Byron's own illicit relationship with Augusta. Manfred is yet another poetic manifestation of the Byronic Hero, a deeply feeling and darkly brilliant social outcast, tormented as much by his own past misdeeds as he is by society's inability to accept and understand him.

As we have seen, the soul of the Byronic Hero is encompassing and capacious, capable of holding within it all of heaven and hell, as Manfred's opening soliloquy indicates: "Sorrow is knowledge: they who know the most / Must mourn the deepest o'er the fatal truth, / The Tree of Knowledge is not that of Life" (1. 1. 10–12). Once again Byron returns us to the great fall, to paradise lost and the consequences of action and experience. Like Satan, Adam, and Prometheus, the Byronic Hero pays a tremendous price for forbidden knowledge, and the resulting suffering makes Manfred at once heroic and tragic, attractive and repulsive. And, as always in the poetry of Byron, these paradoxes are measured in terms of darkness and light. In open defiance of the very spirits he has summoned, the tormented Manfred could assert that

> The mind, the spirit, the Promethean spark,
> The lightning of my being, is as bright,
> Pervading, and far-darting as your own,
> And shall not yield to yours, though coop'd in clay!
> (1. 1. 154–157)

The Fall has not dimmed the inner brightness of the man, just obscured it in a fleshy mantle of clay. Even though a mere mortal, Manfred claims kinship with the immortal, asserting that the light within him shines as bright as that of any transcendent spirit.

But this inner spark is always mediated, muted by the flesh, by a bodily existence that is all the more frail because transient. Manfred's spirits are creatures of air and not subject to the laws of time and decay. But Manfred knew, as did Byron, that the end of all flesh was darkness, oblivion, and death. It is this awareness that makes the Byronic Hero such a conflicted figure, for even amid the beauty of the natural world, the true province of fallen humanity, he can never be truly at home:

> How beautiful is all this visible world!
> How glorious in its action and itself;
> But we, who name ourselves its sovereigns, we,
> Half dust, half deity, alike unfit
> To sink or soar ... (1. 2. 37–41)

Ultimately unfit to sink or soar, but capable at times of both. An eternal outcast, neither pure light nor utter darkness, the Byronic Hero straddled the existential void, with one foot bathed in light and one foot lost in shadow. This almost Sibylline liminality allowed the Byronic Hero to serve as a sort of mystic, a poetic interpreter between the temporal and the spiritual realms:

> The stars are forth, the moon above the tops
> Of the snow-shining mountains. —Beautiful!
> I linger yet with Nature, for the night
> Hath been to me a more familiar face
> Than that of man; and in her starry shade
> Of dim and solitary loveliness,
> I learned the language of another world. (3. 4. 1–7)

And, as with prophets of every age, the price to be paid for such revelation was alienation and isolation.

By November of 1816, Byron had taken up a comfortable residence in Venice, where the congenial climate and relaxed mores afforded his passions every license. He quickly began an affair with Marianna Segati, the wife of his landlord, and he would later boast that he had enjoyed the favors of a different woman on 200 consecutive nights. In 1817, Byron toured Rome and Florence, stopping off in Ferrara, where he visited Ariosto's tomb and Tasso's cell. The latter visit inspired Byron to write "The Lament of Tasso," a moving poem based on the Italian poet's consuming love for Leonora d'Este and his subsequent imprisonment at the hands of Leonora's brother, Duke Alfonso II. Once again, Byron responded deeply to a life of excruciating torment and dazzling achievement, and it is impossible to dissociate Tasso's fictionalized experiences from his own:

> It is no marvel—from my very birth
> My soul was drunk with love, which did pervade
> And mingle with whate'er I saw on earth;
> Of objects all inanimate I made
> Idols, and out of wild and lonely flowers,
> And rocks, whereby they grew, a paradise ... (6. 149–154)

As always for Byron, such idyllic scenes are fleeting in a fallen world and give way to suffering, as these bright remembrances are continually contrasted by the darkness of Tasso's cell and the melancholy of the poet's own mind: "Yet do I feel at times my mind decline, / But with a sense of its decay" (8. 189–190).

During the years 1818 and 1819, Byron threw himself into the festivities of Carnival with reckless abandon and continued his sexual indulgences with Italian women, contracting gonorrhea along the way. The sale of Newstead Abbey in the autumn of 1818, which solidified his finances and alleviated a major source of concern, seemed also to remove the last vestiges of personal restraint governing Byron's conduct. It was at this time that he met and began a scandalous affair with Teresa, Countess Guiccioli, raising eyebrows by actually living for a time with Teresa and her husband. Byron's newfound personal and financial liberation triggered fresh creative insights, and this was a period of great poetic achievement. It can be argued that "The Lament of Tasso" marked a turning point of sorts in Byron's literary career. Although he would never abandon altogether the brooding poetic conventions that gave birth to the Byronic Hero, he began to devote increasing energy to the creation of that exuberant and satirical brand of poetry that became the hallmark of his later years, beginning with *Beppo* (1819) and culminating in his great masterpiece *Don Juan*, which would occupy him from 1819 until his death in 1824.

Byron wrote *Beppo* in *ottava rima*, a lively and spirited verse form that he would subsequently perfect in *Don Juan*. In *Beppo* Byron brilliantly adapts this form to a playful, mock-heroic satire of Italian and English life. The poem chronicles a love triangle that emerges between Beppo, a merchant adventurer who spends long stretches of time at sea, Laura, his lonely and restless wife, and a "cavalier servente," or gentleman in waiting, whom she takes up with to comfort her in Beppo's absence. The playful satire and graceful versification are evident in the account of Laura's decision to take a companion in her husband's absence:

> And Laura waited long, and wept a little,
>   And thought of wearing weeds, as well she might;
> She almost lost all appetite for victual,
>   And could not sleep with ease alone at night;
> She deemed the window-frames and shutters brittle,
>   Against a daring house-breaker or sprite,

And so she thought it prudent to connect her
With a vice-husband, *chiefly* to *protect her*. (1. 29. 225–232)

In tone and style, if no longer in verse form, Byron imitates his poetic
mentor Alexander Pope, whose masterpieces *The Dunciad* and *The
Rape of the Lock* Byron greatly admired. Like Pope and Swift, Byron
creates satire and humor by juxtaposing the sublime and the
ridiculous, the great and the small, in order to expose human vice and
folly.

In September 1818, Byron followed up his success with *Beppo* by
undertaking what would become his greatest work, the ambitious and
comic mock epic *Don Juan*. In Byron's hands, Don Juan, the notorious
lothario of legend, is transformed into a naïve, unsophisticated young
man whose peregrinations expose him to a range of human
experiences and character types. The convention of the innocent hero
and the picaresque nature of the poem recall both Fielding's *Tom Jones*
and Voltaire's *Candide*, as does the emphasis Byron places on Don
Juan's sexual coming of age. If we consider *Childe Harold's Pilgrimage*
as the *terminus a quo* of Byron's career (and the birthplace of the Byron
Legend), it is possible to view *Don Juan* as the *terminus ad quem*. Both
works have semi-autobiographical qualities, incorporating many of
Byron's own experiences into the narrative, but, as we have seen,
Harold the reckless and jaded libertine is very much the "anti-Juan."
Byron makes us aware of Harold's highly developed carnal nature and
amorality from the moment we meet him, whereas Juan somehow
manages to maintain a native innocence and moral compass despite
the numerous "adult" situations in which he repeatedly finds himself.

In Canto I of *Don Juan*, we can see much of Byron's early life in
the unfolding tale of Juan, whose debauched father dies unexpectedly,
leaving the boy his sole heir. Despite a classical education intended to
fit him for higher contemplations, the sixteen-year-old Juan is
seduced by Julia, the wife of his mother's newest lover, Don Alfonso.
After some highly comic machinations, Don Alfonso discovers Juan in
his wife's chambers, whereupon Juan's mother Inez decides to send
her son on a journey to see the world. In successive cantos, Juan is
shipwrecked and sold into slavery in Constantinople. After escaping,
he joins the Russian army, where he distinguishes himself and gains
the notice of Catherine the Great, who sends him to London on a

diplomatic mission, thus reversing, in some small measure, the course of Byron's own self-imposed banishment. And, as in *Tom Jones* and *Candide*, the satire and comedy of *Don Juan* are enhanced by the seemingly static moral nature of the hero as he undergoes his strange journey. This is in some sense the inverse of what happens in epic proper, where the seemingly static nature of the protagonist confers heroism in the face of a shifting and hostile universe. Thus Don Juan serves as the "straight man" in Byron's mock epic, his light illuminating the darkness of human sin, folly, and ignorance that surrounds him.

Although a mock epic, *Don Juan* is still epic in scope and theme, providing us with Byron's most expansive expression of humanity's place in the universe. Harold Bloom sees the poem as "a satire of European Man and Society" that became "Byron's equivalent to Wordsworth's projected *Recluse*, Blake's *Milton*, Shelley's *Prometheus*, and Keats's *Hyperion*. As each of these attempt to surpass and, in Blake's and Shelley's poems, correct Milton, so Byron also creates his vision of the loss of Paradise and the tribulations of a fallen world of experience."[13]

Despite the sprightly verse and witty treatment of human foibles, this poem, like his others, examines the darkness at the core of human experience, and the Fall of Man, both structurally and thematically, occupies center stage:

> But sweeter still than this, than these, than all,
> Is first and passionate love—it stands alone,
> Like Adam's recollection of his fall;
> The tree of knowledge has been pluck'd—all's known—
> And life yields nothing further to recall
> Worthy of this ambrosial sin, so shown,
> No doubt in fable, as the unforgiven
> Fire which Prometheus filch'd for us from heaven.
>   (1. 127. 1019–1016)

Once again Byron returns to Adam and Prometheus (with Satan lurking in the background) for his archetypal images of light and dark. It is perhaps typically Byronic that Juan's first experience of passion is linked to Adam's quest for knowledge and Prometheus' attempt to bring light to a dark world in distinctly sexual terms, an association that Bloom finds shallow: "Imaginatively this is an unfortunate passage, as it reduces both Man's crime and the Promethean theft from the level of disobedience, which is voluntaristic, to that of sexuality itself, a natural endowment."[14] But Byron was aware of the perils of choice in *Don Juan*, and he could apply them to his own calling as poet:

> Nothing so difficult as a beginning
> In poesy, unless perhaps the end;
> For oftentimes when Pegasus seems winning
> The race, he sprains a wing, and down we tend,
> Like Lucifer when hurl'd from heaven for sinning;
> Our sin the same, and hard as his to mend,
> Being pride, which leads the mind to soar too far,
> Till our own weakness shows us what we are. (4. 1. 1–8)

Both passages fuse Judeo-Christian and Classical imagery in typically Byronic fashion to make essentially the same point, that our brightest accomplishments verge always on the darkest impulses, even as Pegasus becomes conflated with Icarus and Lucifer is transformed into Satan. Or, in the words of the critic George Ridenour: "Whether it was the result of the Calvinistic influences on Byron's Scottish childhood, whether it was temperamental, aesthetic, the product of his own experience, or any combination of these factors, Byron seems throughout his life to have had peculiar sympathy with the concept of natural depravity."[15]

Byron would continue to work on *Don Juan* throughout the last few years of his life, years as turbulent as anything his imagination could conjure up for Juan. He continued his high-profile affair with Teresa, who would eventually leave her husband, and began affairs with peasant women and beautiful boys. In the early 1820s Byron was drawn into Italian politics, and his connections with Teresa's family led to his initiation into the Carbonari, a secret society aimed at the overthrow of Austrian rule in Italy. By August 1821, the political situation had become perilous for Byron, who moved to Pisa to distance himself from trouble and to be close to Shelley. In 1822, Byron, Shelley, and Leigh Hunt edited the radical journal *The Liberal*, which carried on even after the drowning of Shelley in July. Byron's interest in politics intensified in 1823, and he was elected to the London Greek Committee, where he took an active part in the cause of Greek liberation from the Ottoman Empire, going so far as outfit a Greek fleet for service with his own money. Sailing to Greece in his ship, *Hercules*, Byron spent his last year engaged in the cause of Greek emancipation, spending great sums of money and expending great resources of energy on a chivalric and romantic enterprise worthy of Conrad in *The Corsair*. In February 1824, Byron experienced what appeared to be an epileptic seizure that seriously weakened him. Despite constant attention from his doctors, who seemed to stabilize his condition, Byron slipped into a coma on April 18, dying the next day.

During the final years of his life, Byron continued to write, expanding *Don Juan* and experimenting with verse drama, producing such works as *Sardanapalus* and *Cain*. But for Byron, action had become as important as poetry, and his last glorious act on the Greek seas further blurred the distinctions between Byron and the Byronic Hero. In death, he was celebrated as a hero and a champion of liberty across the Greek islands, and parts of his body, including his internal organs, were removed as relics and souvenirs. Despite his fame and accomplishment, however, scandal dogged Byron even in death, and his corpse was ultimately denied burial by the deans of St. Paul's and Westminster. In a conversation with Lady Blessington, Byron had once remarked: "Now, if I know myself, I should say that I have no character at all ... But joking apart, what I think of myself is, that I am so changeable, being everything by turns and nothing long.—I am such a strange *mélange* of good and evil, that it would be difficult to describe me." It is precisely this inability to pin Byron down, the indefinable and shifting essence of his character, that fostered and sustains the myth of the Byronic Hero. And it is ultimately this *mélange* of good and evil, this light and dark, that best typifies the man and his poetry. Byron himself expressed it best in *Childe Harold*:

> Yet Time, who changes all, had altered him
> In soul and aspect as in age: years steal
> Fire from the mind as vigour from the limb;
> And life's enchanted cup buy sparkles near the brim. (III. 8. 6–9)

NOTES

1. For a complete account of Byron's life, see Leslie A. Marchand's three-volume *Byron: A Biography* (New York: Knopf, 1957).

2. From the July 6, 1824, entry in the diary of John Cam Hobhouse.

3. All citations of Byron's poetry are from *Lord Byron: The Complete Poetical Works*, Jerome J. McGann, ed. (Oxford: Clarendon Press, 1980).

4. This quote is taken from the collected edition of Byron's correspondence, *Byron: A Self Portrait*, Peter Quennell, ed. (New York: Humanities Press, 1967): 392.

5. See Bernard A. Hirsch's essay "Byron's Poetic Journal," in *Approaches to Teaching Byron's Poetry*, Frederick W. Shilstone, ed.(New York: Modern Language Association of America, 1991): 103.

6. *Byron: A Self Portrait* (London: J. Murray, 1950): 567.

7. All citations of Milton's poetry are from *Paradise Lost and Paradise Regained*, Christopher Ricks, ed. (New York: Signet Classics Edition, 2001).

8. *Lord Byron: The Complete Poetical Work*s, Volume III, 224.

9. See John Clubbe, "Between Emperor and Exile: Byron and Napoleon 1814–1816," in *Journal of Napoleonic Scholarship 1997:* Volume 1, Number 1.

10. *Byron: A Self Portrait*, 256–257.

11. See Percy Bysshe Shelley's "Ozymandias" in *The Complete Poetical Works of Percy Bysshe Shelley*, Neville Rogers, ed. (Oxford: The Clarendon Press, 1975), line 11.

12. See Sir Philip Sidney's "Sonnet 7" from *Astrophil and Stella* in *The Poems of Sir Philip Sidney*, William Ringler, ed. (Oxford: The Clarendon Press, 1962), line 4.

13. *Lord Byron's Don Juan*, Harold Bloom, ed. *Modern Critical Interpretations Series* (Chelsea House: New York, 1987): 1.

14. Bloom, ed.: 4.

15. See George M. Ridenour, "A Waste and Icy Clime" in *Lord Byron's Don Juan*, Harold Bloom, ed. *Modern Critical Interpretations Series* (Chelsea House: New York, 1987): 16.

ROBERT F. GLECKNER

Hebrew Melodies *and* Other Lyrics of 1814–1816

There has probably been more disagreement over the quality of Byron's lyric poetry than over any other kind of poetry he wrote.[1] The case against it is admirably stated by Ernest de Selincourt. The best of Byron's lyrics, he writes, have, "doubtless, a vigour and a colour of their own, but how poor and obvious is their music beside that of Shelley or Keats, Tennyson or Robert Bridges! Byron sets his emotion to a familiar, almost hackneyed, tune: the true lyrist, even if he accepts a conventional framework, weaves upon it his own melody, of which every cadence seems responsive to the finer shades of his emotion." Byron has, De Selincourt concludes, "no magical power over words, no subtlety in verse-music. Hence, though no poet ever succeeded more fully in the expression of himself, he never succeeded in the lyric...."[2] Northrop Frye explains the problem this way: the lyrics in general contain "nothing that 'modern' critics look for: no texture, no ambiguities, no intellectual ironies, no intensity, no vividness of phrasing, the words and images being vague to the point of abstraction."[3] And Eliot blamed all on Byron's "imperceptiveness ... to the English word" and "a defective sensibility."[4]

Although there are no rousing defenses of Byron's lyric talent—indeed few defenses at all for his corpus of lyric poetry—one cannot conveniently and easily ignore L.C. Martin's careful and intelligent lecture entitled "Byron's Lyrics," in which the very shortcomings or

From *Byron and the Ruins of Paradise* (Baltimore: The Johns Hopkins Press, 1967): 203–224. ©1967 by the Johns Hopkins Press. Reprinted with permission of The Johns Hopkins University Press.

85

lacks that Frye and Eliot note are seen as at least potential virtues. In the best lyrics, Martin suggests, "the style is simple without *simplesse*.... Byron can write with [an] avoidance of cliché and [a] reliance upon bare emotive phrasing" that produce an impressive and moving poetry in its own right—what he calls in another connection a "bare but grand sufficiency in style."[5] Herbert Read noticed the same quality, which he describes as an "explicit felicity" of expression: "no image, no word, is far-fetched," and often there is deliberately "the obvious cliché."[6]

Whether or not one agrees with these apologia; whether or not we see a fundamental lack of what Read calls "grace" in the lyrics;[7] whether or not, as Leigh Hunt says, Byron "wanted faith in the interior of poetry";[8] and whether or not he lacks that "something in the mere progress and resonance of the words" that Swinburne thought all great poetry should have, "some secret in the very motion and cadence of the lines, inexplicable by the most sympathetic acuteness of criticism,"[9] Byron's lyric poetry is an integral part of his developing vision and must be examined, to do it full justice, in the evolving context of his total canon.

I

The earliest of the *Hebrew Melodies* in date of composition is the famous and exquisite "She Walks in Beauty." As an anthologist's delight, however, it is always read in isolation, out of its proper context. Byron was certainly aware that, like "Oh! Snatched Away in Beauty's Bloom" and "I Saw Thee Weep," the song was no Hebrew melody. Their apparently disruptive and inconsonant inclusion in the volume I take as evidence that the themes of the tales and their pessimistic view of the human condition were never far from Byron's mind no matter what the immediate occasion for poetry or the immediate stimulus to write. In the context of the whole of *Hebrew Melodies*, "She Walks in Beauty" takes on aspects of the Edenic sections of the tales: "All that's best of dark and bright" meet in the figure of woman,

> Thus mellowed to that tender light
> Which Heaven to gaudy day denies.

Though severely underplayed, the clash between "tender" and "gaudy" should not be overlooked, nor the fact that "Heaven" bestows the perfection. The by now familiar Byronic duality of mind and heart is here fused in an other-worldly light, poised supernaturally above "all below," innocence not yet seared by the world's fierce conflict. "She" is *not* merely Lady Wilmot, about whom the poem was ostensibly written, but rather Woman—or mankind; and if the inspiration was a ball at Lady Sitwell's,[10] one can marvel at Byron's superb control and craft in fashioning the occasional *vers de société* to his own ends. (The thematic picture is even more complete if, adopting the technique of the insistent biographizers, we discover that Lady Wilmot was dressed in mourning at the time of the party[11]—Byron's vision of death in life par excellence.)

This opening poem is immediately followed in the collection by an unusual hymn to the immortality of sound and poetry, "The Harp the Monarch Minstrel Swept," in which music and poetry are equated with a lost heaven: the sounds of David's harp, grown "mightier than his Throne," "aspired to Heaven and there abode!" But now on earth "its chords are riven," and man is left with only the desperate hope that that "bursting spirit" will "soar" again

> To sounds that seem as from above,
> In dreams that day's broad light can not remove.[12]

But it is only in dreams, as we have seen, that music soars and valleys ring—in dreams or, at best, in a lost past recalled now through ruins or through song. In such a world death is inviting. As Keats wrote, luxuriating in the immortal song of the nightingale,

> Now more than ever seems it rich to die,
>   To cease upon the midnight with no pain,
>   While thou art pouring forth thy soul abroad
>   In such an ecstasy—

so Byron writes in "If That High World," "How sweet this very hour to die—but *only* if "there the cherished heart be fond, / The eye the same, except in tears." If one could only be sure of immortality, it would indeed be sweet

> To soar from earth and find all fears
>   Lost in thy light—Eternity!

"It must be so," says man's conscious mind, for sanity demands the dream that gives us respite from our thoughts of death; let us therefore channel the mind toward that dream:

>   let us think
> To hold each heart the heart that shares,
> With them the immortal waters drink,
>   And soul in soul grow deathless theirs!

The syntax is crabbed and obscure, but the forcefulness of the exhortation to believe that all hearts are those that share belies the conviction that the second stanza ostensibly conveys. Like "Israel's scattered race" in the superb "The Wild Gazelle," all hearts are doomed to "wander witheringly" further and further from "scenes of lost delight," until in death they find, not peace, but eternal exile, misery, and separation:

> And where our fathers' ashes be,
>   Our own may never lie;

"And Mockery sits on Salem's throne." As in all of the tales, but perhaps especially in *The Prisoner of Chillon*, nature is indifferent—and different—at once providing both a foil for man's misery and enslavement and an illusory escape from that condition. Thus while the Jews had "Inhabitants more fair" than the stately gazelle, "Judah's statelier maids are gone" and

> The wild gazelle on Judah's hills
>   Exulting yet may bound,
> And drink from all the living rills
>   That gush on holy ground;
> Its airy step and glorious eye
> May glance in tameless transport by.

So too, while Israel's scattered tribes "must wander witheringly," the palm tree remains

In solitary grace:
It cannot quit its place of birth,
It will not live in other earth.

For Byron the homeless Jews wandering in strange lands, whom not even death can reunite, are symbolic of man[13]—just as the modern Greek, enslaved and cowed, is also man. Since slavery, exile, and death have become synonymous with life, man can only be mourned, as in "Oh! Weep for Those," "By the Rivers of Babylon We Sat Down and Wept," and "By the Waters of Babylon." Amid the general mourning, however, there are occasional notes of defiance and hope, perhaps even more striking because of the general gloom surrounding them and their tone of desperation rather than conviction. For example, in "Thy Days Are Done" weeping is deplored. Yet even here, while hope seems to be sustained, it depends, paradoxically, on the hero, the "chosen Son," who is now dead. To weep would do his glory wrong, and, with a curious Byronic infelicity that may be a studied ambiguity, the dead hero "shalt not be deplored." The battle songs take their cue from this note: it is the "Song of Saul before His Last Battle" that is sung, its martial positiveness severely qualified by Saul's imminent death and by the companion poem, "Saul," in which Death appears *in propria persona* to claim

"Crown less—breathless—headless ...
Son and Sire—the house of Saul!"

Jerusalem is destroyed by Titus and his Roman hordes ("On the Day of the Destruction of Jerusalem by Titus"), and the fist-shaking last stanza of that poem, spoken by one whose home, temple, and God have been lost, simply cannot redeem the time nor call forth the miraculous thunderbolt to "burst on the Conqueror's head!"

Even in victory the cost of battle is immense, and, as in the bullfight and gladiator scenes of *Childe Harold*, Byron's emphasis is ever on the loss rather than the gain. Though Jephtha is victorious over the Ammonites (in "Jephtha's Daughter"), Byron shrewdly makes his daughter the speaker of the poem, emphasizing thereby the essential idiocy of demanding the death of love as the price of victory.

Byron's choice of language in her speech creates an undertone that condemns the God and the human condition that render such sacrifice necessary, and inculcates the sense of horror, not jubilation, with which we are to read the entire poem. Similarly, in the much-acclaimed as well as abused "The Destruction of Sennacherib,"[14] although the forces of "right" win, it is difficult to ignore Byron's emphasis on the loss, the waste, and the horror inherent in the slaughter of the Assyrians. It is as if all nature died in this landscape of death, the final victory hollow and wintry. The Assyrian horde descends on "the fold" like wolves (reminiscent of the jackals, hyenas, and wild dogs of *The Siege of Corinth*), and the Lord's triumph is seen as tantamount to the coming of winter's blasts, bringing not life but the breath of the "Angel of Death," awakening "the sleepers" from their dream of life to the "deadly and chill" reality of eternal darkness. The "glance of the Lord" surveys not a new world, or even victory, but a wasteland where steed and man lay "distorted and pale"—

> And the tents were all silent—the banners alone—
> The lances unlifted—the trumpet unblown

—all life destroyed at its moment of awakening.[15]

Apart from the awkward Elizabethanism of "I Saw Thee Weep," then, all of the *Hebrew Melodies* are hymns to loss, elegies, celebrations of victories without triumph, prophecies of doom, or landscapes of despair. Even the so-called love poems, which do not seem to fit the over-all theme of the volume, reflect similar attitudes and states of mind.[16] "Oh! Snatched Away in Beauty's Bloom," which H. W. Garrod sees as a rare "perfect lyrical whole"[17] points out that "tears are vain," that "Death nor heeds nor hears distress," and that the dead past lives indelibly in memory as a grim force in the present. Man who is left alone, without love, wanders eternally, his soul dark, with only poetry and music for release and relief. In "'All Is Vanity, Saith the Preacher,'" Byron reasserts the lack of peace or hope even in memory, for as the speaker of that poem tries to recall days he would wish to live over, he finds that

> There rose no day, there rolled no hour
>   Of pleasure unembittered;

> And not a trapping decked my Power
> That galled not while it glittered.

In the lines Byron wrote originally to follow these, the unrelieved darkness of his vision evinced itself in a picture of the eternity of man's woe, the impossibility of change in the world and in the human condition:

> Ah! what hath been but what shall be,
> The same dull scene renewing?
> And all our fathers were are we
> In erring and undoing.[18]

No spell or art, neither wisdom nor music, can lure the serpent thought from round the heart. For Byron, as man in the large consistently represents Adam fallen and Christ crucified, in small, he is the heart eternally stung and galled. Here is no mere melancholy, stagey or otherwise, but rather a considered despair that is not alleviated even in his conception of immortality. In one of his rare poems on the subject, "When Coldness Wraps This Suffering Clay," the mind, as usual with Byron, is seen as immortal, leaving "its darkened dust behind." What is striking about his vision, however, is its lack of humanity, its void, even while the mind encompasses all in its passionless and pure eternity. Terrifyingly like its counterpart, the "suffering clay" that is doomed to wander the earth in a vain search for peace and paradise, the "Eternal—boundless—undecayed" but also "unembodied" mind strays amid the stars, uncircumscribed by time or space or history, yet "Fixed in its own Eternity." Soaring above all humanity and earthly things, it is also above humanity's love and hope, and exists "A nameless and eternal thing" lost in the void. Such "freedom" is only the freedom of Bonivard extended to infinity, the universe of Manfred, which gives the final lie to the aspiring hope of suffering clay—what Byron in "A Spirit Passed Before Me" calls succinctly "all formless—but divine."

Byron's views of immortality remained unusually consistent throughout his life, and they constantly reflect, as in *Hebrew Melodies*, his uncomfortable relationship with God. The will to believe is always there: his heart will have it so, but his mind denies it and his experience only serves to corroborate his doubt. "It is useless," he writes in his *Detached Thoughts*, "to tell me *not* to *reason*, but to *believe*. You might as well tell a man not to wake but *sleep*."[19] In the context of Byron's deliberate fusion of the darkness of dreams and the darkness of reality in the poems of 1815 to 1816 studied in the previous chapter, his use of the same terms here is especially significant. If doubt and faith are equally real, the latter (the dream) is the less real to the extent that it is what we wish, not what is. Ultimately, of course, the mind triumphs, steeling itself against the heart's desire and hope and thus destroying any sense of God as a meaningful presence in the universe. Deistically, for Byron, "a *Creator* is a more natural imagination than a fortuitous concourse of atoms."[20] Realistically, experience tells him that Christianity is absurd: "It is a little hard to send a man preaching to Judaea, and leave the rest of the world— Negers and what not—*dark* as their complexions ... and who will believe that God will damn men for not knowing what they were never taught?"[21] Again, in his journal, his heart reaches out to accept God, but his mind cancels the gesture: "... let me live.... The rest is with God, who assuredly, had He come or sent, would have made Himself manifest to nations, and intelligible to all."[22]

Byron's incipient deism, then, is simply a convenient device for imagining creation. Unlike the deist's divine mechanism whose perpetual motion is governed by immutable laws and whose central truth is that whatever is, is right, Byron's created universe, in perpetual motion but governed by no apparent laws, is instinct with the central truth that whatever is, is painful. It is a world torn religiously by sects which in turn tear "each other to pieces for the love of the Lord and hatred of each other,"[23] torn politically by man in his lust for the power of godhood, torn socially by stratification and hypocritical self-righteousness, and torn morally by the very laws geared to maintain its peace and well-being.

Eternity or immortality for Byron is, somewhat curiously, both mental and material. The mind, an organ of "perpetual activity" which acts often "very independent of body,"[24] is man's immortality; but whereas even in the privacy of his journals he will not speculate on how far that future life "will at all resemble our *present* existence,"[25] in "When Coldness Wraps This Suffering Clay" he does see it as at least analogous to worldly wandering, a parallel chaos. On the other hand, if "Matter is eternal, always changing, but reproduced, and, as far as we can comprehend Eternity, Eternal,"[26] then why not man, this suffering clay? We are miserable enough in this life," he writes to Hodgson, "without the absurdity of speculating upon another. If men are to live, why die at all? and if they die, why disturb the sweet and sound sleep that 'knows no waking'?"[27] Thus man's immortality exists in the eternity of his mind as well as in the perpetuity of what Byron calls "the congregated dust called Mankind."[28] Yet he sees both eternal mind and mankind as doomed to sorrow, tragedy, and death, or at best to perpetual lonely wandering. "It cannot die, it cannot stay," he writes of the "immortal mind" in "When Coldness Wraps This Suffering Clay"; its existence is a continual fluctuation or dizzying pendulum swing between the extremes of mortality and immortality, or, in the language of the tales, between heart and mind, love and hate, peace and war, life and death. It is certainly because of this intense sense of life's violence and uncertainty, its irony and perverseness, that Byron can say, on occasion, and certainly with more conviction than in his other pronouncements upon life, love, God, and man, "Like Sylla, I have always believed that all things depend upon Fortune, and nothing upon ourselves"[29]—much less upon a God who may or may not have really "come" or "sent."

II

The other lyric poetry written about the same time as *Hebrew Melodies* is the most autobiographical of all, and one must strongly resist the temptation to tie it to specific occasions or personal circumstances if one is to see there the substantial evidence of the controlling vision in Byron's poetry as a whole.[30] The vanity or impossibility of love in this world is one of the major themes in these lyrics, as it was in *Hours of Idleness*, and is frequently embodied in farewells. "Farewell! If Ever Fondest Prayer" is such a poem, in which "to speak—to weep—to sigh" is vain:

> I only know we loved in vain—
>   I only feel—Farewell!—Farewell!

"When We Two Parted," "I Cannot Talk of Love to Thee," "I Speak Not, I Trace Not, I Breathe Not Thy Name," and "Bright Be the

Place of Thy Soul" are others, relieved only momentarily by "There Be None of Beauty's Daughters." Perhaps most characteristic of the lyrical poems of this period, however, and with interesting echoes of the music, as well as the despair, of *Hebrew Melodies*, are two of those entitled simply "Stanzas for Music" (one beginning "There's not a joy the world can give," the other beginning "They say that Hope is happiness"). Of the first Byron wrote flippantly to Moore that he felt "merry enough to send ... a sad song," but the genuineness of its sentiment is attested to by his two other letters to Moore (one written six days later than the above, one a year later[31]) and his elegy "On the Death of the Duke of Dorset." The sudden death of Dorset, a friend from Harrow days, set Byron to "pondering, and finally into the train of thought which you have in your hands."[32] It is a crucial train of thought for our purposes here, for it describes the beginnings of a turning point in Byron's poetic career.

Ever since the youthful lyrics of *Hours of Idleness* and the arrogant abusiveness of *English Bards and Scotch Reviewers*, Byron's vision of the world and man, what I have been calling the human condition, has been growing darker and darker. We have seen how, in *The Bride of Abydos*, for example, even wrenching his thoughts away from reality by plunging into fantasy merely led him to picture a fantasy grimmer than the reality from which he sought relief. There is considerable significance, then, in the step he takes in "My Soul Is Dark" of the *Hebrew Melodies*: poetry, at least in his conscious dealings with it, has ceased to be an escape from reality's dark dream and has become instead a means for expressing his grief and despair. His earlier (1813) image of its being "the lava of the imagination whose eruption prevents an earthquake" has been transformed from image to reality. For the issue now, in 1815 to 1816, is no longer escape: even death and a possible immortality hold no certain rest. The issue is that of one's sanity in the face of what inevitably must be, the discovery of the means by which the heart (and hence essential humanity) can endure the constant attacks upon its very sanctuary. In "My Soul Is Dark" that heart, doomed now to know the worst, will "break at once" if it does not, or cannot, "yield to song"; now the lava must flow lest the earthquake destroy that last refuge of man, the world of his mind.

Yet the very expression of grief, personal or universal (for they are one and the same for Byron), can soon become unbearable; the bleeding heart runs dry; the elegies become increasingly powerless to preserve the mind's sanity. To harden one's heart, to become in a sense less than human (as so many of the heroes in the tales do), to gain life and sanity at the expense of feeling—or at the very least to evolve a poetic point of view and construct sufficient to support such self-discipline—is the logical step for Byron the man and poet to take. Canto III of *Childe Harold* is the first major product of this turn: Harold himself deems

> his spirit now so firmly fixed
> And sheathed with an invulnerable mind,
> That, if no joy, no sorrow lurked behind.
>
> (x)

And in the superb stanzas on the death of "young, gallant Howard" and all the myriad slain at Waterloo, we are told that

> There is a very life in our despair,
>   Vitality of poison,—a quick root
>   Which feeds these deadly branches; for it were
>   As nothing did we die; but Life will suit
>   Itself to Sorrow's most detested fruit.
>
> (xxxiv)

Without steeling the heart, it "will break, yet brokenly live on,"

> Even as a broken Mirror, which the glass
>   In every fragment multiplies—and makes
>   A thousand images of one that was,
>   The same—and still the more, the more it breaks;
>   And thus the heart will do which not forsakes,
>   Living in shattered guise; and still, and cold,
>   And bloodless, with its sleepless sorrow aches,
>   Yet withers on till all without is old,
> Showing no visible sign, for such things are untold.[33]
>
> (xxxiii)

But such control is evinced in other ways as well, as the evolution of the creative poet in *Childe Harold* III and IV shows. The mind is more than a controller of the heart; it is also a creator of a brave new world, of life that is, paradoxically, more intense, of a new heart—but only so long as self is dissociatable from creation:

> 'Tis to create, and in creating live
>   A being more intense that we endow
>   With form our fancy, gaining as we give
>   The life we image, even as I do now—
>   What am I? Nothing: but not so art thou,
>   Soul of my thought! with whom I traverse earth,
>   Invisible but gazing, as I glow
>   Mixed with thy spirit, blended with thy birth,
> And feeling still with thee in my crushed feelings' dearth.
>
>   (III, vi)

Thus the mind's creativity, as well as its vain control, re-creates life and feeling, and, perhaps most important, preserves man's sanity amid desolation.[34] But if that creativity and control can sustain, through a philosophy of art, the essential lyricism of *Childe Harold* even through the fading of those visions and the sinking of that spirit in Canto IV, it can also, with what Byron learned in his struggle for a structure and mobile point of view in the tales, produce beings more intense, more dramatic in conception, who live and love and fight and die in a world whose limits are history and whose integrity as inviolable, independent creatures, divorced yet not divorced from their creator, is assured by their historical truth or their mythological reality. Or that mind can inure itself against its own agony by laughing so that it may not weep, by seeing the horror of the human condition as comically absurd. Thus Beppo lands at Venice and, as in all fairy tales, reclaims "His wife, religion, house, and Christian name" (*Beppo*, xcvii); there is no final cataclysm as in *The Siege of Corinth*, where Alp remains a renegade to the end and the top blows off the universe in a climax reminiscent of MacLeish's "The End of the World." King George III slips into heaven unnoticed at the conclusion of what must be called, for sanity's sake, "this true dream" (stanza cvi), the farcical and brilliant *The Vision of Judgment*. And in *Don Juan* Byron makes the point explicit a number of times:

No more—no more—Oh! never more, my heart,
    Canst thou be my sole world, my universe!
Once all in all, but now a thing apart,
    Thou canst not be my blessing or my curse:
The illusion's gone for ever, and thou art
    Insensible, I trust, but none the worse,
And in thy stead I've got a deal of judgment,
    Though heaven knows how it ever found a lodgement;

                           (I, ccxv)

and, with direct reference to the somberness of *Hebrew Melodies*,

So Juan wept, as wept the captive Jews
    By Babel's waters, still remembering Sion:
I'd weep,—but mine is not a weeping Muse;

                           (II, xvi)

and, most revealing of all,

    if I laugh at any mortal thing,
    'Tis that I may not weep; and if I weep,
'Tis that our nature cannot always bring
    Itself to apathy, for we must steep
Our hearts first in the depths of Lethe's spring,
    Ere what we least wish to behold will sleep:
Thetis baptized her mortal son in Styx;
A mortal mother would on Lethe fix.

                           (IV, iv)

In such a world, when laughter is not possible (for example, at the madness and death of Haidée), the poet can always force himself into flippancy:

But let me change this theme, which grows too sad,
    And lay this sheet of sorrows on the shelf;
I don't much like describing people mad,
    For fear of seeming rather touch'd myself—
Besides, I've no more on this head to add.

                          (IV, lxxiv)

A "capricious" muse is all he'll have, a main character from legend, and "The monde" (XIV, xix), whose "grand arcanum" is "not for men to see at all" (xxii). "And therefore what I throw off is ideal" (xxii); the facts that the same mind cannot afford to admit are facts, the secret horrors of life that, once revealed, must not be acknowledged as such.

The "train of thought" that Byron mentions to Moore as having been aroused by his contemplation of the death of Dorset is this very steeling and hardening that the creation of poetry makes possible— the defensive posture of the psyche that finally calls an urgent halt to the perpetual fragmentation of the heart. On hearing of Dorset's death Byron can say "I heard thy fate without a tear," even though his friend was "surpassing dear, / Too loved of all to die." Instead, dry tears fall "dreary" on his heart,

> dull and heavy, one by one,
>   They sink and turn to care,
> As caverned waters wear the stone,
>   Yet dropping harden there:
> They cannot petrify more fast.
>   Than feelings sunk remain,
> Which coldly fixed regard the past,
>   But never melt again.

Byron brilliantly universalizes this particular loss in the first "Stanzas for Music" mentioned above, a poem which by its very title and nature describes the turning point I spoke of earlier. It is simultaneously the poet's cry for music and song to prevent the earthquake of mind and his recognition that such a public vent of emotion is no longer sufficient to guarantee the mind's equipoise:

> There's not a joy the world can give like that it
>   takes away,
> When the glow of early thought declines in Feeling's
>   dull decay.

The visions of Eden that inform and characterize the boy too young to know the irrevocability of its loss and therefore blindly persistent in his attempts to recover it reveal themselves here with double force as a panorama of ruin:

the few whose spirits float above the wreck
                                        of happiness
Are driven o'er the shoals of guilt or ocean of excess:
    The magnet of their course is gone, or only points
                                        in vain
The shore to which their shivered sail shall never
                                        stretch again.

Then the mortal coldness of the soul like Death itself
                                        comes down;
It cannot feel for others' woes, it dare not dream
                                        its own;
That heavy chill has frozen o'er the fountain of
                                        our tears,
And though the eye may sparkle still, 'tis where the
                                        ice appears.

Though wit may flash from fluent lips, and mirth
                                        distract the breast,
Through midnight hours that yield no more their
                                        former hope of rest;
'Tis but as ivy-leaves around the ruined turret wreath,
All green and wildly fresh without, but worn and
                                        grey beneath.

If "midst the withered waste of life" tears *could* fall, they would be sweet; but the poet knows too that even that sweetness is illusion, the sweetness of residual pain after torture ceases, for the springs found in deserts only *seem* sweet because of their real brackishness (stanza v).

In the second "Stanzas for Music" ("They say that Hope is happiness"), the vision is even darker; both hope and memory are lost,

And all that Memory loves the most
    Was once our only Hope to be,
And all that Hope adored and lost
    Hath melted into Memory.

Time future and time past fuse in the desert of present ruins:

> Alas! it is delusion all:
>   The future cheats us from afar,
> Nor can we be what we recall,
>   Nor dare we think on what we are.

When Byron writes to Moore in early 1816 that "There's Not a Joy" is "the truest, though the most melancholy, [poem] I ever wrote,"[35] it is impossible to dismiss this judgment as another of his offhand indiscriminate remarks. Melancholy's shadow has lengthened into despair; the "wandering outlaw of his own dark mind" has become the fully mature poet, aware now of his own vision, and urgently needing a control, a form, a technique by which to cope with that vision (Byron calls it in one of his poems to Augusta "that deep midnight of the mind"[36]).

The other alternative for the aware man is, of course, death, and it must be admitted that to Byron that possibility of eternal rest and peace is powerfully seductive.

> Count o'er the joys thine hours have seen,
>   Count o'er thy days from anguish free,
> And know, whatever thou hast been,
>   'Tis something better not to be,

he wrote as early as 1812 in "Euthanasia." Still, like Shelley and Keats, Byron saw the prospect of death as not without its risks and uncertainties. All three could only be "half in love with easeful death," for the possibility of utter extinction to Shelley and Keats weighed equally in the scales with their visions of eternal peace, love, and beauty. For Byron, as we have seen in *Hebrew Melodies*, death might also be an eternal lonely vigil in the exile of spacelessness and timelessness. Further, to yield weakly to the archetypal tyrant was for him the final slavery, the surrender of the will and dominion of the mind. The hymn to Prometheus is thus both a lament for archetypal man's sentence of eternal life—

> Titan! to thee the strife was given
>   Between the suffering and the will,

> Which torture where they cannot kill;
> And the inexorable Heaven,
> And the deaf tyranny of Fate,
> The ruling principle of Hate,
> Which for its pleasure doth create
> The things it may annihilate,
> Refused thee even the boon to die

                                                         (ii)

—and a paean of praise for his "impenetrable Spirit, / Which Earth and Heaven could not convulse." Prometheus is the epitome of man's

> firm will, and a deep sense,
> Which even in torture can descry
> Its own concentered recompense,
> Triumphant where it dares defy,
> And making Death a Victory.[37]

Man's eternal conflict is not merely between his dust and deity, but also between his will and suffering, between his mind and fate. If defeat, man's "funereal destiny," as Byron called it in "Prometheus," is inevitable, the quality of his resistance is the measure of his stature and the exercise of his godhood. That resistance is his ultimate and only freedom, whereas suicide or the life of a captive is his final surrender. Even so, the choice is not so simple. Bonivard's indomitable will only leads him to love his prison and to give thanks for a world of mice and spiders over which he may rule as monarch. Thus his final "freedom" is the universal prison and slavery of the "free" world.

The poems to Napoleon of 1814 to 1816, the most outspoken of which is the *Ode to Napoleon Buonaparte*, reflect the same dilemma. After completing *The Corsair* Byron had promised Murray no more poetry, but Napoleon's abdication of the "throne of the world" made it "physically impossible to pass over this damnable epoch of triumphant tameness."[38] What is important about the poem is that it is not political. Byron had always been stirred by Napoleon's greatness, as well as aware of his tyranny:

The sword, the sceptre, and that sway
Which man seemed made but to obey.

                                                                (iv)

The epithets liberally sprinkled through the *Ode* reveal his continued
ambiguity of attitude: he is the tyrant "who strewed our earth with
hostile bones" (i), one of "Those Pagod things" (iii), a "Desolator,"
"victor," and "Arbiter of others' fate" (v), an "All Evil Spirit" and "a
thing so mean" (ix), a madman who arose "To shame the world" (xi),
"a throneless Homicide" (xiii), a "Timour" (xv), a Prometheus (xvi).[39]
Byron's anger is not for any of these, nor for Napoleon's "surrender,"
nor is the poem a call for the renewal of tyranny and slaughter. Rather,
it is an attack upon Promethean man for yielding meekly to the world
and its prison. He is now "a nameless thing" (i), an "Ill-minded man"
(ii) whose self-destruction is a scourge to man's potential greatness,
whose "dread of death alone" led him to the "ignobly brave" choice of
living a slave rather than dying a prince (v):

> It is enough to grieve the heart
>   To see thine own unstrung;
> To think that God's fair world hath been
> The footstool of a thing so mean.

                                                                (ix)

The lesson of the poem is at least twofold: with Napoleon's fall
"mortals" can finally see "Ambition's less than littleness" (ii):

> Thanks for that lesson—it will teach
>   To after-warriors more
> Than high Philosophy can preach,
>   And vainly preached before.
> That spell upon the minds of men
> Breaks never to unite again,
>   That led them to adore
> Those Pagod things of sabre-sway,
> With fronts of brass, and feet of clay,

                                                                (iii)

but they can also see, alas, that even history's most Promethean spirits,
however warped and contemptuous of mankind, however perverted by

lust for power, settle sadly for a breathing ignominy rather than a defiant death. Out of such an attitude comes, two years later, the triumphant heroism of *Manfred*, as well as the surrender of Cain.

NOTES

1. Byron is rarely given credit for his extraordinary range of poetic and metrical experiments. As De Selincourt reminds us, few poets experimented more than he: "romance, descriptive and lyrical, drama—monologue—song: in octosyllabic and heroic couplets, Spenserian stanza, blank verse—and a great variety of lyrical measures" (*Wordsworthian and Other Studies*, p. 121).

2. *Ibid.*, pp. 106–7.

3. "George Gordon, Lord Byron," p. 152.

4. "Byron," in *On Poetry and Poets*, p. 201 (reprinted from *From Anne to Victoria*).

5. The Byron Foundation Lecture, published as *Byron's Lyrics* (Nottingham, 1948), pp. 10, 13.

6. *Byron* (London, New York, and Toronto, 1951), p. 24; *The True Voice of Feeling* (New York, 1953), p. 307.

7. *Byron*, p. 24,

8. *Lord Byron and Some of His Contemporaries* (2 vols.; London, 1828), I, 78.

9. *Miscellanies*, p. 127.

10. The circumstances of the poem's composition are found in a manuscript note by James Wedderburn Webster on Byron's letter to Webster of 11 June 1814, in *LJ*, III, 92n.

11. *P*, III, 381n.

12. In manuscript the last six lines of the poem are even more unequivocally negative:

> It there abode, and there it rings,
>> But ne'er on earth its sound shall be;
> The prophets' race hath passed away;
>> And all the hallowed minstrelsy
> From earth the sound and soul are fled,
>> And shall we never hear again?

(P, III, 383n)

13. Marchand, in one of the few intelligent commentaries on *Hebrew Melodies*, will not go quite this far, but he does isolate two main themes in the work, "the deep pathos of the loss of Eden, the wait of a wandering and homeless people, and ... the battle cry of Jewish Nationalism. The lost Eden

was easily identified in Byron's feelings with the general romantic lament for lost innocence and beauty" (*Byron's Poetry*, p. 134). At the other extreme from Marchand's sensitive reading is Sir Arthur Quiller-Couch's wholesale and imperious condemnation of the entire volume as "turgid school-exercise work," in an essay which trails throughout the red herring of Byron's "sincerity" or "insincerity" ("Byron," in W. A. Briscoe [ed.], *Byron, the Poet* [London, 1924], p. 10; first published in *Studies in Literature*, 2d ser. [Cambridge, 1922]). What is more surprising, perhaps, is the total neglect of *Hebrew Melodies* in two of the most recent attempts to study Byron as a poet, those of Andrew Rutherford (*Byron: A Critical Study*) and M. K. Joseph (*Byron the Poet*).

14. E.g., G. Wilson Knight thinks that "in short space [it] condense[s] almost all the main values of Byron's weightier, tragic and religious, genius" (Review of W. W. Robson's *Byron as Poet*, *Essays in Criticism*, IX [19591, 88); Martin calls it "the apex, the crown of Byron's lyrical writings" (*Byron's Lyrics*, p. 15); and Marchand sees it "rightly admired as one of Byron's most musical lyrics. It is a tour de force but a brilliant one with perfect blending of mood and meter.... it transcends the alliterative and anapestic and sound-association devices and even the common melodramatic theme and captures the imagination and feelings of anyone sensitive to music and poetry" (*Byron's Poetry*, p. 135). On the other hand, Samuel C. Chew describes it, I think accurately, as "famous but overrated" (Lord Byron: "Childe Harold's Pilgrimage," p. 488n).

15. Despite the radically different circumstances, "Herod's Lament for Miriamne" may be seen as a variation on the same theme; indeed, with but slight change, it can be read as Jephtha's answer to his daughter's brave speech of farewell, except that in this case it is the tyrant Herod who grieves over his killing of love (see especially ll. 13–24). The similarity between this relationship and its destruction to the history of the lovers in the tales and "The Dream" is striking.

16. Only Marchand has commented on this extraordinary unity of tone and theme. Although he excludes "She Walks in Beauty" (erroneously, I think), he sees in all the love songs the same "haunting sadness and the sense of desolation which inform the poems voicing a wild lament for the lost Jewish homeland" (*Byron's Poetry*, pp. 133–34).

17. *Byron, 1824–1924* (Oxford, 1924), pp. 18–19.

18. *P*, III, 395n.

19. *LJ*, V, 457. The italics are Byron's.

20. *Detached Thoughts*, in *LJ*, V, 459. The frequently quoted ltr. to Ensign Long of 16 Apr. 1807 ("I have lived a *Deist*, what I shall die I know not") hardly "proves" Byron a consistent deist throughout his life, as some critics have averred. The letter is found in *LJ*, II, 19–20n.

21. Ltr. to Hodgson, 3 Sept. 1811, in *LJ*, II, 21.

22. *Ibid.*, pp. 22–23.

23. *Ibid.*, p. 22.

24. *Detached Thoughts*, in *LJ*, V, 457.

25. *Ibid.*

26. *Ibid.*, p. 458.

27. Ltr. of 3 Sept. 1811, in *LJ*, II, 18–20. Byron quotes Seneca to clinch his point, emphasizing the negative in the last line:

> Post mortem nihil est, ipsaque mors nihil
>
> . . . .
>
> Quaeris, quo jaceas post obitum loco?
> Quo non nata jacent.

28. *Detached Thoughts*, in *LJ*, V, 458.

29. *Ibid.*, p. 451.

30. Happily, the inveterate biographizing of the poems in recent years has yielded to controversy over the critical propriety and usefulness of biographical evidence in studying Byron's poetry. But even now it is rare to find analyses of the poetry and a conviction that it can be read without biographical assistance. If Patricia Ball can assert that "it is possible to get nearer to the poems by leaving aside the problems of the Byronic personality altogether" ("Byronic Reorientation," *The Twentieth Century*, CLXVIII [1960], 328), and W. W. Robson can flatly demand that "the assessment of Byron's poetry ... must begin and end with the poetry" ("Byron as Poet," p. 30), the loudest voices are still those of such critics as Patrick Cruttwell and Paul West. The latter not only wrote a book (*Byron and the Spoiler's Art*) in which all of Byron's poetry is seen as a function of his need to "eliminate" but also wrote, in another place (*Introduction to Byron: A Collection of Critical Essays* [Englewood Cliffs, N. J., 1963], pp. 1–2, 10–11):

> To try excluding the man is eventually to discover that little of the poetry can stand alone and, if it is made to, seems like fragments from the hands of various pasticheurs.... He obtrudes, and he sabotages the "text-only" kind of study.... It is no use reorganizing and tabulating the works of this scintillating and uncomfortable man. Byron is now not the celebrity or the hot issue he used to be; so, unfortunately, the academic feels safer in trying to systematize and factorize the restless quality of the poems.

And Cruttwell says, ironically enough in reviewing West's book, that it "fails because that poetry just will not, cannot stand up by itself. It has to lean on the letters and journals, and they on the man behind them; and if interest of that sort is vulgar, is unliterary, so be it: for Byron, it is the only interest" ("Romantics and Victorians," *Hudson Review*, XIV [1961–62], 602). In a sense this study is intended to refute, at least in part, the Cruttwells and the Wests.

31. Ltrs. to Moore, 2 and 8 Mar. 1815 and 8 Mar. 1816, in *LJ*, III, 181, 183–86, 272–75.

32. Ltr. to Moore, 8 Mar. 1815, in *LJ*, III, 183–84.

33. Cf. what Byron may have said to Lady Blessington—or what may be her plagiarism of this passage: "Memory, the mirror which affliction dashes to the earth, and, looking down upon the fragments, only beholds the reflection multiplied" (*Conversations of Lord Byron*, p. 177).

34. For excellent but differing interpretations of this crucial stanza in Byron's development as a poet, see, e.g., Ridenour's dissertation, "Byron and the Romantic Pilgrimage," *passim.*; Pafford's "Byron and the Mind of Man"; and Wasserman's *The Subtler Language*, pp. 6ff. (a very brief but acute analysis). Harold Bloom's interpretation of the stanza as Byron's affirmation of "a therapeutic aesthetic idealism" is, I think, very misleading (*The Visionary Company*, p. 234).

35. Ltr. of 8 Mar. 1816, in *LJ*, III, 274.

36. "Stanzas to Augusta," beginning "When all around grew drear and dark."

37. For somewhat different interpretations of this poem (which Arnold and many of his followers saw, and is still seen by some, as Byron's "typical" poem, an example of his "titanism"), see especially Ridenour's *The Style of "Don Juan"* and Bloom's *The Visionary Company* (the latter's promisingly titled essay, "Napoleon and Prometheus: The Romantic Myth of Organic Energy," in *Yale French Studies*, XXVI [1960–61], 79–82, is notably unhelpful). H. J. C. Grierson sees "Prometheus," curiously, as Byron's "'Everlasting No'" ("Lord Byron: Arnold and Swinburne," *Proceedings of the British Academy*, IX [1920], 16).

38. Ltr. to Moore, 20 Apr. 1814, in *LJ*, III, 70.

39. The ambiguity can further be seen in the University of Texas manuscript of the poem, to which Coleridge did not have access. For example, in stanza ix, for "Evil Spirit" Byron originally wrote "Evil greatness," and in stanza xi, for "Some new Napoleon" he wrote first "Some other madman."

JEROME J. McGANN

The Book of Byron and the
Book of a World

Byron wrote about himself, we all know, just as we all know that his books, like God's human creatures, are all made in his image and likeness. This quality of his work is apparent from the very beginning. His first book, *Fugitive Pieces*, was privately printed in 1806 for an audience of friends and acquaintances who were privy to its local references and biographical connections—many of which were connections with themselves. *Hours of Idleness*, his first published work, appeared the following year, and it sought to extend the range of Byron's intimacies to a somewhat larger book purchasing audience. In *Hours of Idleness* Byron projected himself before his English audience as a recognizable figure whom, he trusted, they would be happy to take to their breasts. In *Hours of Idleness* the English world at large met, for the first time, not the Man but the Lord of Feeling, a carefully constructed self-image that was fashioned to launch him on his public career. This was not conceived, at the time, as a literary career.[1]

Byron succeeded in his effort, though not precisely as he had expected. Certain hostile reviews—most notoriously, Brougham's in the highly visible and influential *Edinburgh Review*—interrupted Byron's initial, unruffled expectations. Had he reflected more critically on the hostile reception that *Fugitive Pieces* had provoked in

From *Critical Essays on Lord Byron*, edited by Robert F. Gleckner (New York: G.K. Hall & Co., 1991): 266–284. First appeared in *The Beauty of Inflections*, ©1985 by Jerome J. McGann. Reprinted by permmission of Oxford University Press and the author.

certain narrow quarters of its local (Southwell) society, he might have anticipated some trouble for his next book.[2] But he did not, apparently, and seems only to have realized later that he was destined to be both the darling and the demon of his age.

The attack on *Hours of Idleness* was another opportunity for Byron to produce yet a third Book of Himself: this time, *English Bards and Scotch Reviewers*, the fiery counter-attack on his persecutors and the culture that supported such beings (*CPW*, 1:398–99). If it is true that Byron was "born for opposition," this book revealed that fact, for the first time unmistakably.

And so it went on. In 1809 Byron left benighted England to chew over the high rhetoric of his last book, and he plunged into Europe and the Levant, where his next productions began to accumulate their materials in the much larger context of European affairs. He wrote a continuation, or sequel, to *English Bards and Scotch Reviewers* called *Hints from Horace*, which was not published in his lifetime, and he composed the first two cantos, of that unsurpassed act of literary self-creation, *Childe Harold's Pilgrimage: A Romaunt* (*CPW*, 1:426–27, 2:268–71).

This book is worth pausing over—not the poem, but the book.[3] It is a handsome and rather expensive (30*s.*) quarto volume beautifully printed on heavy paper. It comprises four distinct parts: (1) the title poem in two cantos (pp. iii–109); (2) the extensive notes to these cantos (pp. 111–61); (3) a section headed "Poems" that included fourteen short pieces (pp. 163–200); (4) an appendix containing bibliographical materials, translations, Romaic transcriptions, and one facsimile MS, all having to do with the current state of the literary culture of modern Greece (pp. 201–[27]). Its publisher conceived its audience to be a wealthy one, people interested in travel books and topographical poems, people with a classical education and with a taste for antiquarian lore and the philosophical musings of a young English lord. As it turned out, all of England and Europe were to be snared by this book's imaginations. It went through a dozen (cheaper) editions in three years and established all of the principal features of that imaginative (but not imaginary) world-historical figure known as Byron. Later circumstances would only provide the public with slightly different perspectives on this figure.

The book of *Childe Harold* published in 1812 picks up the autobiographical myth that Byron had left *in medias res* when he left

England in 1809.[4] The notes specifically recall the controversy surrounding *English Bards and Scotch Reviewers*, the section of "Poems" is so arranged as to mirror the personal tale narrated through the title poem, and the latter presents a dramatic picture of a young lord who leaves his local home and friends, as well as his country, in a condition of psychic and cultural alienation. Simply, he is disgusted with himself and the world as he has thus far seen it. He finds, when he flees to other lands and in particular to the fabulous Levantine seat of western culture, that his own personal anomie, experienced in the tight little island of Britain, mirrors the condition of Europe (or, in Byron's startling and important variation on this ancient topos, that Europe and the entire world mirrors his personal condition). Thus does Byron force himself—and the individual person through himself—to the center of attention. What his book says is not simply that we should deplore the condition of western culture in this critical time, but that we should deplore it because its debasement has poisoned its chief, indeed, its only, value: the individual human life. In particular, Byron's life.

Byron inserts his personal history into the latest phase of the European crisis that began in 1789. The outbreak of the Peninsular War in 1809 initiated the last act in the drama of the Napoleonic Wars, which would end in the defeat of Napoleon and the restoration of the European monarchies under the hegemony of England. In *Childe Harold* (1812) Byron's itinerary takes him first to the very heart of the Peninsular events, where his initial mood of disgust at his English existence acquires its European dimensions. When he moves to the East and the dominions of the Turkish Empire, including Greece, his cynicism is confirmed: Greece, the very symbol of the west's highest ideals and self-conceptions, lies in thrall not merely to the military rule of the Porte but to the contest of self-serving political interests of the English, French, and Russians.

This is the context that explains Byron's peculiar appendix, with its heterogeneous body of Romaic materials. *Childe Harold* (1812) is obsessed with the idea of the renewal of human culture in the west at a moment of its deepest darkness. This means for Byron the renewal of the value of the individual person, and the renewal of Greece as an independent political entity becomes Byron's "objective correlative" for this idea. *Childe Harold* (1812) is thus, on the one hand, a critique of present European society and politics and, on the other, a pronouncement of the crucial need throughout Europe for the independence of Greece. As Byron would later say: "There is no freedom—even for Masters—in the midst of slaves."[5] The question of Greece thus becomes for Byron a way of focusing the central questions that bear upon the present European epoch. The Europeans normally date this epoch from 1789, and rightly so, but in this book (as well as in his next two books, *The Giaour* and *The Bride of Abydos*), Byron argues that the conflict of European self-interests can be best and most clearly understood in terms of the recent history of Greece, whose abortive efforts for independence in the late eighteenth century were either neglected by the European powers or actively betrayed.

Thus, in *Childe Harold* (1812) Byron enlarged his personal myth, which he had already begun to develop in his earlier books, by inserting it into the wider context of the European political theatre as it appeared to him in 1809–1812. The central ideological focus of the entire myth involves the question of personal and political freedom in the oppressive and contradictory circumstances that Byron observed in the world of his experience. More than anything else this book says that the most personal and intimate aspects of an individual's life are closely involved with, and affected by, the social and political context in which the individual is placed. Byron goes further to say that such a context is more complex and extensive than one ordinarily thinks, that each person is more deeply affected by (as it were) invisible people, places, and events than we customarily imagine. Ali Pacha and his Albanians may appear far removed from England and the Napoleonic Wars, but to the perspicacious European they will have more than a merely exotic interest. Similarly, Byron's rather ostentatious use of antiquarian and classical materials is not merely a clumsy display of learning and artistic pedantry. On the contrary, Byron invokes the classical world and the later history of Europe's investment in that world because this complex ideological and political network impinges directly upon current European affairs and hence on the experience of each single person living in Europe. A powerful and illuminating irony runs through Byron's flight from contemporary England and Europe and his pursuit of ancient Greek ideals:

> Of the ancient Greeks we know more than enough; at
> least the younger men of Europe devote much of their
> time to the study of Greek writers and history, which
> would be more usefully spent in mastering their own. Of
> the moderns, we are perhaps more neglectful than they
> deserve; and while every man of any pretensions to
> learning is tiring out his youth, and often his age, in the
> study of the language and of the harangues of the Athenian
> demogogues in favour of freedom, the real or supposed
> descendants of these sturdy republicans are left to the
> actual tyranny of their masters.... (p. 143)

Byron's proposal in his book is to look at England, Europe, and
Greece, not as these political entities appear in their ideological self-
representations, but "as they are" (p. 144) in fact. The reality reveals
an Islam and a modern Greece very different from what they are
commonly represented to be in English and European commentaries;
it also reveals the hypocritical fault lines that run through the high-
minded and Greek-derived ideologies of liberty to which the major
European powers give lip-service. In Byron's book, the image of the
young European gentleman acquiring a classical education is
contradictory and deeply satiric. Such a person's mind is filled with
self-congratulating and self-deluding ideas that permit him to identify
with the dream of ancient Greece even as they also allow him to
remain blind to certain important actualities: that the Russians "have
twice ... deceived and abandoned" the Greeks; that the French seek
"the deliverance of continental Greece" as part of their policy for "the
subjugation of the rest of Europe"; and that the English, in addition
to the pursuit of their economic self-interests, profess to seek the
freedom of Greece even as they subjugate the rights of "our Irish
Helots" (p. 161) and "Catholic brethren" (p. 143).

In Byron's books—*Childe Harold* (1812) is merely prototypical in
this respect—the variety of materials often conveys an image of
heterogeneity, but in fact this image is no more than the sign of
intrinsic connections that are not normally perceived, of connections
between "opposite and discordant" matters that only *appear* to be
separated but that are in fact fundamentally related. The soon-to-be-
published Oriental Tales are not merely a set of exotic adventure

stories. They constitute a series of symbolic historical and political meditations on current European ideology and politics in the context of the relations between East and West after the breakup of the Roman Empire and the emergence of Islam.[6] That later readers and critics have often taken Byron's Levantine materials as a sign of a (presumptively shallow) poetic interest in local color and oriental ornamentation merely testifies to a failure of critical intelligence and historical consciousness. Byron was deeply interested in these social and political questions and he used his poetry to probe their meaning and their roots. Later criticism has too often translated *its* disinterest into a myth of the intellectual poverty of Byron's verse.

Byron's skill at manipulating his publications produced some of the strangest and most interesting books of poetry ever printed in England. *The Giaour* may stand as one example out of many.[7] Like the other tales that were soon to follow, this poem is a political allegory told from the point of view of those "younger men of Europe" whom Byron described in the notes to *Childe Harold* (1812). The subject of the poem, at the plot level, is the state of modern Greece around 1780. At the narrative level, the poem is a contemporary (1809–13) meditation on the meaning of the European (and especially the English) understanding of Levantine politics between 1780 and 1813. The poem's story (its plot level) is a nihilistic tragedy in which all parties are involved and destroyed. The meditation on the story is carried most dramatically in the introductory 167 lines, which appear as the "original" work of the poem's redactor (Byron himself), as well as in the poem's "Advertisement" and its many prose notes, also represented in *The Giaour* as the "original" work of the editor/redactor Byron. The entire significance of this excellent work does not appear unless one responds to the interplay between the poem's two "levels." Briefly, the "original" work of the editor/redactor comprises a set of deeply contradictory materials: on the one hand, a complete romantic sympathy with the characters and events as well as an absorption in the heroic ideology that they exhibit; on the other, a mordant series of comical remarks on Eastern mores and commonplace European ideas about such matters. This radical split in the poem's attitude at its meditative level reflects back upon, and interprets, the European understanding of the Levant between 1780 and 1813. The interpretation that Byron produces is a critical one: the

European understanding is self-deluded and helpless, and Byron's own exposure of this failed understanding is represented as the one-eyed man's vision in the kingdom of the blind. The comedy of the poem's notes, apparently so urbane, is in fact a flinching away, the laughter, spoken of in *Don Juan*, that serves to hold back weeping and bleaker realities.

All of Byron's works, and especially his published books, exhibit intersections of these kinds. Thus, his bibliography is more than a scholar's guide and resource, it is as well a graphic display of his life in books and of the extension of his life through books. The piracies, the huge number of translations, the numerous printings all attest and perpetuate the poetic explorations of reality that he initially set in motion. And it is the "books," rather than the "poems" (or least of all the "texts"), that draw attention to the central quality of Byron's poetical work; for when we study the works through their material existences we are helped to see and understand the social and historical ground that defines their human meanings.

Nowhere is this fact about Byron's work more clear than in the case of his masterwork, *Don Juan*. We respond to its name as if it were one thing, as indeed it is; but it is also, like the world it expresses and represents, incredibly various and polyglottal. Readers have of course always responded to that variety, but we must do so even as we also bear in mind that the variety is of a determinate and specifiable sort. *Don Juan* is, formally, a romantic fragment poem comprising six authorized and published volumes, along with a body of material that was not published until after Byron's death, at different times and with various justifications. The first two volumes were published by John Murray in a certain way, and the next four volumes were published by John Hunt in a very different way. Important aspects of the meaning of the poem are bound up with these interesting events in the work's publication history.[8]

Most important to see is that when Byron began publishing the poem with John Hunt he was released from certain constraints that he had to struggle against when he was publishing with the conservative house of Murray. *Don Juan*'s (rejected) preface and (suppressed) dedication emphasize the political and social critique that is finally so fundamental to the poem.[9] But Murray and his allies forced Byron to revise the published version of the first five cantos so as to *de-*

emphasize this aspect of the epic. As a consequence, the original cantos 1–5 (the first two published volumes of the poem) preserve the poem's social and political critique as a peripheral and subsidiary matter, an incidental topic that seems to appear and disappear in the poem in a random way. The suppressed dedication was not published until 1832, and the rejected preface did not appear until 1901.

With the appearance of cantos 6–8, published by Hunt, the situation changes radically. These cantos are introduced with a prose preface where the social and political issues are finally raised to a great, even to a dominant, position; and the poetic materials as well undergo a shift in emphasis toward more explicitly social and political matters. This change in the poem has been recognized for some time and critics have described the differences between the earlier and the later cantos in various (often useful) ways. What has not been seen, however, is the structural change brought about in the poem as a whole when Byron began his epic "again" (as it were) with cantos 6–8 and John Hunt.

We can begin to see what is involved here by looking briefly at the original preface to cantos 1–2. Byron never completed this preface, which descends to us in his fragmentary draft MS. Nevertheless, what he did complete gives us some interesting information about Byron's initial conception of his work. In the course of satirizing Wordsworth, Byron tells his readers that "the following epic Narrative" is to be regarded as the work of a certain "Story-teller" who is living, and delivering his narrative, at a certain place and time: specifically, "in a village in the Sierra Morena on the road between Monasterio and Seville" sometime during the Peninsular War (the reference to the village in the Sierra Morena is autobiographical and specifies the date as 1809). As for the narrator himself, "The Reader is ... requested to suppose him ... either an Englishman settled in Spain—or a Spaniard who had travelled in England—perhaps one of the Liberals who have subsequently been so liberally rewarded by Ferdinand of grateful memory—for his restoration" (*DJV*, 2:4–5). This passage establishes a second point of view on the events treated in the poem: that is, one subsequent to 1814 and the early years of the period of European restoration following the fall of Napoleon. As it turns out, the reader inevitably places this historical vantage point at that moment of contemporaneity that attaches to the poem's date of composition and/or publication (in this case, 1818–19).

Byron finally dropped his preface with its specific historical perspectives, and he did not fully exploit the structural advantages of his poem's double perspectivism until he began to reconceive the project of *Don Juan* in 1822–23. Before considering that act of reconception, however, we should reflect upon the double historical perspective in terms of which the work was initially conceived and set in motion. Like the later cantos, cantos 1–5 organize their materials in two dialectically functioning historical frames of reference: on the one hand, the frame of the poem's plot or "story," which contains the narrated events of Juan's life; and, on the other hand, the frame of the poem's narrating voice, which comprises Byron speaking to his world between 1818 and 1824 via the six published volumes of *Don Juan*. Byron's rejected and incomplete preface to cantos 1–2 reminds us that he initially had some idea of using the plot level and the narrative level to comment on each other and that he thought of Juan's life in specific historical terms. As it turned out, he rejected the idea of setting the poem's narrative frame in the complicated way suggested by the initial preface, where it is unclear whether the narrator speaks from the vantage of 1809 or 1818, or both. In cantos 1–5 Byron also neglected to specify clearly the historical frame in which Juan's career is placed. When he published cantos 6–8 with John Hunt, however, he finally let his contemporary readers see very clearly the exact relation between the history of Juan's career and the history of the poem's narrator, Byron *in propria persona*.

We can date Byron's reconception of his epic fairly exactly: in January and February 1822, which is the period when Byron resumed his composition of *Don Juan* (he left off his poem when he finished canto 5 at the end of 1820). Byron wrote to Murray on 16 February 1821 (*BLJ*, 8.78) and outlined a projected plot for Juan's adventures. This outline, however, only corresponds in a loose and general way to the episodes of the poem that he was soon to write and hence shows that Byron had not yet fixed on a definite plan. Byron first articulated this plan to Medwin between December 1821 and March 1822:

> I left him [Juan] in the seraglio. There I shall make one of
> the favourites, a Sultana ... fall in love with him, and carry

him off from Constantinople.... Well, they make good their escape to Russia; where, if Juan's passion cools, and I don't know what to do with the lady, I shall make her die of the plague.... As our hero can't do without a mistress, he shall next become man-mistress to Catherine the Great.... I shall ... send him, when he is *hors de combat*, to England as her ambassador. In his suite he shall have a girl whom he shall have rescued during one of his northern campaigns, who shall be in love with him, and he not with her.... I shall next draw a town and country life at home.... He shall get into all sorts of scrapes, and at length end his career in France. Poor Juan shall be guillotined in the French Revolution! What do you think of my plot? It shall have twenty-four books too....[10]

This scheme corresponds fairly closely to the poem as we now have it, and it holds to the general plan that Byron gave to Murray at the beginning of 1821 (though not to the particular details of the episodes). The most important episode missing from Byron's outline is the siege of Ismail, though it is clear from this and Byron's immediately preceding discussion that he planned to send Juan into war. But in the first few months of 1822 Byron seems not yet to have decided on the Ismail episode, as he had not yet worked out how to separate Juan and Gulbeyaz. These decisions would be made in the next few months. The idea of having Juan die on the guillotine in the French Revolution was certainly fundamental to the plot of the poem from the earliest stages of its conception as a plotted sequence.

The preface to cantos 6–8, written in September 1822, calls attention, on the one hand, to the historical immediacy of the poem as it is Byron's act of discourse with his world and, on the other, to the specific (past) historical nexus in which Byron's story of Juan's career is imbedded. The second part of the preface is a bitter diatribe against Castlereagh, who had recently taken his own life, against the present condition of Europe under the restored thrones and their allied policies, and against those like Southey who were at once supporters of these institutions and detractors of Byron's recent work. The opening sentences of the preface, on the other hand, tell us that the material in cantos 7 and 8 is based upon an actual event: the siege of

Ismail by the Russians in November–December 1790. The latter was the chief episode in the (latest) Russo–Turkish War, which had been renewed in 1787. The preface tells the reader, in other words, that Juan's career in Byron's poem is unfolding within real historical time, and—specifically—that we are to map his career in terms of specific places, dates, and events. When Juan goes to Catherine's court after the siege of Ismail, the date is early 1791. Shortly afterwards he goes to England.

Clearly, then, Byron's projected scheme for the plot of Juan's career was actually being implemented when Byron renewed the poem's composition at the beginning of 1822. That he was preparing Juan for a trip to Paris and death on the guillotine in 1793 at the end of the poem is borne out by the fulfillment of the other details that he gave to Medwin, as well as by the chronology of Juan's exploits established in the siege of Ismail episode.[11] We should note that this precise dating of Juan's life in the poem accommodates itself to the events of cantos 1–6. Byron had not, before the preface to cantos 6–8, forced his audience to read the events of cantos 1–6 within a specific historical frame of reference. After the preface, however, those events are drawn into the poem's newly defined historical scheme. Juan's life in Byron's poem begins in Seville just as the French Revolution has broken out, or is about to break out. His life will end at the end of Byron's poem, and the date for him will be 1793.

Lacking the precise historical frame that Byron established for his poem in 1822, Juan's career would appear episodic, the verse equivalent of the fictional careers of characters in Smollett, Sterne, and Fielding.[12] The exact historical placement changes the situation dramatically. Juan at first appears to move through Byron's poem in a picaresque fashion, but as the poem develops and his life is brought into ever-closer relations with the great and epochal events shaking Europe in the early 1790s, the reader begins to glimpse an order, or perhaps a fate, that was not at first evident or even suspected. Having Juan die in the Reign of Terror at the end of Byron's poem is a daring conception: on the one hand, it seems a surprising, even an arbitrary, end for Byron's inoffensive hero, but, on the other, it calls attention to a hidden constellation of forces drawing together far-flung and apparently unrelated people and events. History proceeds "according to the mighty working" of forces that gather up the odd and the disparate, and historical explanation, in Byron, proceeds according to the mighty working of a poem that *reveals* these odd and unapparent connections.

Not least of all does it reveal the connections that hold between the pan-European world of 1787–93 and its counterpart in 1818–24. The revolutionary epoch in which Juan's career begins and ends is explicitly examined from the vantage of the period of Europe's restoration. Juxtaposing these two worlds allows each to comment on the other. More crucially for the poem, however, the juxtaposition gives Byron the opportunity to expose certain congruences between these periods and to suggest that the second period is a variant repetition of the first. These congruences are established via the third historical frame that gives a structure to *Don Juan*: the period in which the Book of Byron was initially composed, and more especially the central years of that period, 1809 to 1817/18.

The congruences appear most dramatically as a series of related and repeating sequences of gain and loss, rise and fall, triumph and disaster. Juan's career illustrates this pattern both in its particular episodes and in the larger scheme that Byron projected for his hero. Adversative forces of various kinds interrupt and thwart Juan's plans and hopes. Some of these are represented as his responsibility while others originate in external circumstances over which he can have no control. In both cases, the pattern of an early promise that later fails or is betrayed appears in Juan's life as well as in the course of the French Revolution. Juan's life follows the moral arc of the revolution even as his career follows its early chronological development. But what is most important, so far as Byron's poem is concerned, is that both of these sequences recur in the next generation. The second phase of the revolution is dominated by the rise and fall of Napoleon, whose professed aim (at any rate) was to establish the revolution on a secure European footing. The consequence of his career was, on the contrary, the final defeat of the revolution's historic agenda. This repetition, in Napoleon's life, of the historical course of the early years of the revolution appears in Byron's poem through its autobiographical analogue: the meteoric rise and subsequent fall of Lord Byron, a series of events that we—following Byron—associate with the years 1809–1817/18. In Byron's and Napoleon's careers the reader of *Don Juan* observes, once again, the pattern established in Juan's life and in the course of the early revolution.

Following his self-exile from England in 1816 Byron meditated on the meaning of this pattern in his life and on its relation to similar patterns in past and contemporary history. The most important of these meditations comes down to us as *Childe Harold's Pilgrimage*, canto 4, which Byron completed shortly before he began *Don Juan*. Here Byron decides that all history, when judged by meliorist or revolutionary standards, is a story of disaster and unsuccess. What he also decides, however, is that against this fatal and repeating story may be, and has been, placed the deed of the opposing mind and will, the individual voice which, while it recognizes the evil pattern, refuses to accept or assent to it.

> Yet, Freedom! yet thy banner, torn, but flying,
>   Streams like the thunder-storm *against* the wind;
> The trumpet voice, though broken now and dying,
>   The loudest still the tempest leaves behind. (*CHP* 4, stanza 98)

> Yet let us ponder boldly—'tis a base
>   Abandonment of reason to resign
> Our right of thought—our last and only place
>   Of refuge.... (*CHP* 4, stanza 127)

These attitudes establish the ground on which *Don Juan* comes to judge the patterns of historical repetition. Byron begins the poem from the vantage of 1818, a point in European history when time appears to have rolled back upon itself. Thirty years have passed, yet the enormous upheavals that marked those years seem to have returned the European world virtually to the same political position that it occupied in 1788. Furthermore, Byron observes in this period a series of repetitions that suggest that the cycle of revolutionary disappointment is a general pattern that is found in many historical periods and is replicated for the individual as well as for society. In terms of the narrator's historical frame (1818–24), *Don Juan* is yet another revolutionary undertaking begun in a period of darkness. As such, the bleak patterns of repetition over which the Byron of 1818–24 will brood—the pattern of Juan's career and the early phase of the revolution, the pattern of Byron's career and the Napoleonic wars—threaten the narrative project of 1818–24 with a fearful end.

Byron begins *Don Juan* already knowing that individual and social history, from a revolutionary point of view, always follows a curve of disappointment or disaster. In this sense (but only in this sense) the poem is "nihilistic." In every other respect the poem is a great work of hope, for it insists that projects of change and renewal must continue to be raised up despite the fact of absolute adversity. The Byron who set *Don Juan* in motion understands that the eye begins to see only in a dark time, and—more crucially—that there never is a time that is or was not dark. Those who seek not merely to understand the world, but to change it, strive toward an ideal of human life that will have to be "anywhere out of the world." This is the strife of *Don Juan*'s hope, the deed of its mind—the fact of its books. The poem begins its quest for renewal under its own prophecy of failure, and it seeks to persuade its readers that one begins in this way simply because there is no other place to begin, that the renewal arrives with the event, not in the end. For in the end you lose, always.

Thus Byron begins his poem in 1818 by calling for a new hero to take the place of all the failed heroes of the past and, in particular, of all the failed heroes of the preceding revolutionary epoch. Byron catalogues their names in canto 1 only to toss them aside in favor of "our friend, Don Juan," whose history he purposes to tell. As we have seen, however, and as every reader of the poem has always recognized, that fictive history recollects and alludes, at every point, to the actual history of Lord Byron, who is the poem's true "hero" and central figure. Juan's progress from Seville to the Levant, and thence via Russia to England and (prospectively) to Paris and his death, is shadowed by the actual career of Byron. In fact, Juan's career is no more than a displaced re-presentation of Byron's, a coded fiction through which the reader may glimpse the friends, enemies, and the incidents of Byron's life, as well as the patterns and epochs of that life. The English cantos, at the level of the poem's plot, should be located in the summer and early autumn of 1791; at the level of the poem's recollective autobiographical structure, as everyone knows, these cantos reflect Byron's life in England during his Years of Fame.

When Byron reinitiated his *Don Juan* project at the beginning of 1822, therefore, he did so with two objects clearly in his mind. The first of these involved structural matters: specifying a precise chronology for Juan's life in the poem. This move entailed, as a consequence, a dramatic refocusing of the poem's materials. Because of the move readers would be better able to see the tripartite organization of the poem's historical vision. *Don Juan* examines the period 1789–1824 in terms of its three dominant phases: the early years of the French Revolution (the poem's displaced fiction); the epoch of the Napoleonic Wars (viewed through Byron's analogous and contemporary experience of those years); and the epoch of the European restoration (dramatically fashioned and presented at the poem's immediate narrative level).

Byron's second object, which is related to the first, aimed to reassert in an unmistakable way the socio-political character of his work. When he began *Don Juan* he spoke of it as "bitter in politics" (*BLJ*, 6:76–77), but as he struggled to get Murray to publish his cantos he was gradually led to deemphasize both the bitterness and the politics. The de-emphasis appeared in the published work itself— the removal of the dedication, the decision not to print the Wellington stanzas in canto 3, and so forth—as well as in Byron's letters back to England in which he raised his defense of the poem against his publisher's and his friends' objections.[13] During 1819–21 these letters take a conciliating and mollifying line. Byron tried to get his poem accepted by assuring his friends that it was actually a harmless thing, an elaborate *jeu d'esprit* conceived more in a comic than a satiric mode, "to giggle and make giggle" (*BLJ*, 6:67, 208). In 1822 the structural changes are accompanied by an uncompromising and candid political stance. In his resumed poem, he told Moore in July 1822, he meant to "throw away the scabbard" and make open ideological war with the new reactionary spirit of the age (*BLJ*, 9:191). By December he was equally clear on the subject in a letter to Murray: *Don Juan* "is intended [as] a *satire* on *abuses* of the present *states* of Society" (*BLJ*, 10:68). Cantos 5–8, issued by the liberal Hunt rather than the conservative Murray, are prefaced with Byron's prose declaration of mental war, and the next volume—cantos 9–11—begins with the diatribe against war and Wellington which Byron, in 1819, had withdrawn from canto 3.

Byron's purposes with his poem, then, are accompanied by important changes in his aesthetic and political consciousness. Not the least of these was his new and clearer understanding of the *wholeness* of the period 1789–1824, of the intimate relations that held between the three major phases of this period, and of the connections between people and events that might appear, at first, to have little to do with each other. No episode in the poem reveals more clearly Byron's increased understanding of these historical repetitions and relations than the Siege of Ismail, the episode in which Byron initially focused the historical and political restructuring of his epic.

The siege is, at least in part, what it appears to be: a satire on war and its violence. Byron was not a pacifist, however. He supported patriotic struggles and wars of liberation, and he eventually went to serve in the Greek effort to break free of the Turkish Empire. We have to specify, therefore, the ground of Byron's satire. This ground begins to emerge when we reflect upon Byron's chief source for his details. He used the account in Marquis Gabriel de Castelnau's *Essai sur l'Histoire ancienne et moderne de la nouvelle Russie* (3 vols., Paris, 1800).[14] The ideology of this book is reactionary and monarchist, and its narrative of the siege is largely based on the first-hand details supplied to Castelnau from the diary of Armand Emmanuel du Plessis, Duc de Richelieu (1767–1822). Byron mentions Castelnau's *Essai* in the preface to cantos 6–8, where he also speaks of the Duc de Richelieu as "a young volunteer in the Russian service, and afterwards the founder and benefactor of Odessa" (*DJV*, 3:3). The irony and satire implicit in these remarks arises from Byron's negative approach to Castelnau's glorifying account of the siege, as well as from his ironic sense of the young Richelieu's benefactions.

Reading Castelnau, Byron saw that many of the officers in Catherine's army at the siege of Ismail were "distinguished strangers" (canto 7, line 254), a wickedly oblique phrase calling attention to the fact that these men, like the young Duc de Richelieu, were emigrés from France and the revolution. Richelieu and the other distinguished strangers are not patriots fighting for their country, they are military adventurers. That Byron intended this line of attack on the French emigrés at Ismail is perfectly plain from the letter to Moore in which he said that his new cantos (the siege cantos, that is) constitute an attack upon "those butchers in large business, your mercenary soldiery" (*BLJ*, 9:191). Lying behind the satire of this battle and the entire Russian episode in the poem is the idea, commonly found in liberal thought of the period, that monarchists like Richelieu have no other business in life except to fight in wars (any wars will do) and intrigue at court. The fact that Juan's rescue of Leila is based upon an actual incident in Richelieu's life only underscores Byron's mordant comments on the indiscriminate militarism of aristocratic ideology:

> If here and there some transient trait of pity
> > Was shown, and some more noble heart broke through
> Its bloody bond, and saved perhaps some pretty
> > Child, or an aged, helpless man or two—
> What's this in one annihilated city? (8, stanza 124)

These lines, and the larger passage from which they are drawn, cut back against Castelnau's account of the war and the supposed "noble heart" of the young duke. The man celebrated by reactionaries like Castelnau as "the founder and benefactor of Odessa" is as well one of those who destroyed a city in which he had no personal or political interest whatsoever, who fled his own country at a moment of crisis, and who later—after the fall of Napoleon—returned to France to become minister for foreign affairs in the restored monarchy.[15]

Richelieu merely epitomizes what Byron wishes to attack in his narrative of the siege and in the Russian cantos generally: the character of monarchist regimes. He is even more important in Byron's poem, however, as a focus for the political filiations that connect, on the one hand, such apparently separated events as the siege of Ismail and the events in France in 1789–90 and, on the other, the strange twists and eventualities of European history between 1789 and 1818. Richelieu and the other distinguished strangers do not find their way into Catherine's army merely by chance, nor is it chance that brings him back, at the Bourbon restoration, to serve as an important functionary in the reactionary alliance. Neither is it chance that leads Byron in 1822 to expose this pattern of relations through his narrative of the siege. Byron was well aware, at least since 1809, of the imperialist stake that various European powers had in Balkan and Levantine affairs. The narrative of the siege of Ismail forces the reader to recall to mind that network of political and economic interests, as well as to see that the power and self-interests of the monarchies have not been broken by the revolutionary and Napoleonic years. When Byron looks at the siege from the vantage of the restoration, then, he integrates it into the pattern of pan-

European affairs of 1789–93 (that is to say, the event is integrated into the order and fate of Juan's fictional-historical career), and he also uses it to comment upon current European conditions. In effect, Byron's employment of his sources involves him in a massive critical-revolutionary reinterpretation of the history of Europe from the outbreak of the French Revolution to the early years of the restoration.

Thus, in 1822 Byron transforms *Don Juan* into a book of the European world, a comprehensive survey and explanation of the principal phases of the epoch 1789–1824. The period is dominated by repetitions, by the violence that has accompanied them, and by the ignorance and indifferences that have abetted these repetitions and their violences. Against these things Byron sets the project of *Don Juan*, which is itself finally recognized to be involved in, to be a part of, the epoch and its repetitions. *Don Juan* becomes a book of the European world by becoming, finally, the Book of Byron, an integrated meditation and commentary upon his own life as it is and was and continues to be a revelation of the meaning of his age.

Don Juan is the Book of Byron because he is its hero, because the poem gives the reader a history of 1789–1824 that is set and framed, at all points, in terms of Byron's history. Juan's fictional movements retraverse actual places and scenes that Byron once passed through, and their details recollect persons and events in his past. In addition, the digressive narration often ruminates Byron's career to comment on and finally to judge it. In short, the poem repeatedly gives the reader views of Byron's past life in the coded sequence of its fictional level as well as in the memorial sequence of its narrative level. All this is widely recognized, as is the related fact that the history of an entire epoch is to be glimpsed in the reflective details of the poem.

Less apparent is the significance of the narrative as it is an immediate rather than a recollective event. Cantos 1–5 constitute the fictional level and the narrative level through two volumes of verse issued by John Murray in 1819 and 1821, and the remaining cantos constitute themselves through the four succeeding volumes issued by Hunt in 1823 and 1824. In addition, however, the last four volumes reconstitute what was originally printed in the first two volumes (a) by forcing the reader to place the whole of the fictional level in a specified historical frame of reference, and (b) by making this important interpretive shift a part of the poem's developing structure, a part of its own self-criticism. Byron begins the Hunt volumes of his poem, cantos 6–16, with a preface announcing his ideological purposes and describing the key elements in the historical restructuring of the poem. Cantos 6–16 then carry out these changes of direction and thereby force cantos 1–5 to accommodate the changes. The structural accommodations we have already discussed. The ideological changes appear as a more comprehensive understanding of the subjects taken up by the project of *Don Juan*. Most noticeable here is Byron's effort to present a totalized interpretation and critique of his age: to compel his readers to understand how the several phases of the period 1789–1824 hang together and to persuade them that his critical-revolutionary reading of the period is the correct one. Related to this polemic is the poem's vision of self-judgment, its critical-revolutionary reading of the limits and blindnesses of cantos 1–5. Byron's revisionary turn on the first five cantos is not, of course, a repudiation of them. Though an act of self-criticism, the change of direction in cantos 6–16 assumes— indeed, it demonstrates—a dialectical continuity with its objects of criticism. The advances and the retreats of cantos 1–5, their boldness and timidity, accumulate a set of dynamic contradictions that eventually generate cantos 6–16.

In this way *Don Juan* represents not merely a comprehensive interpretation of the period 1789–1824 but a comprehensive critical interpretation that incorporates its own acts of consciousness in its critique as part of a developing and changing act of interpretation. All readers have recognized this quality of the poem's digressive and shifting style, but it is important to see that this stylistic feature is grounded in the work's ideological structure. Even more important to see, however, is that the ground of this ideological structure is not in some definable form of critical interpretation that we may educe from the work. Rather, it lies in the act of the poem, the social and historical deeds of its consciousness that appear to us, most immediately, as a set of specific acts of publication. Of course, the fragmentary character of the work has heretofore obscured somewhat the comprehensiveness of its historical argument. Scholarship helps to bring that argument into sharper focus, to lift it from the sphere of a reader's intuition into a more explicit and defined frame of reference.

Late in the poem Byron says of himself that like his own work *Don Juan* he is "Changeable too—yet somehow *'Idem semper'*" (17, stanza 11). Readers have not found it easy to say what exactly in the poem is "changeable" and what exactly stands resistant to change. I think we can now make an attempt to isolate these factors. What changes in the poem are its ideas; these are continually subjected to qualification, revision, even repudiation. What remains the same is the perpetual dialectic of the individual mind in its social world, the active deed of its committed intelligence. Fichte called this ground of permanence "Tat," Schopenhauer "Wille." These are of course nothing more than conceptual markers for an act of social consciousness that can only be carried out in words but that cannot be defined in them. The act of the poem's mind, then, is an understanding that changes and brings about change. In Don Juan— to adapt a contemporary formulation of a fragment from Herakleitos—"What does not change / is the will to change."[16]

NOTES

1. For a discussion of these matters see my *Fiery Dust: Byron's Poetic Development* (Chicago: University of Chicago Press, 1968), chap. 1, and *Lord Byron: Complete Poetical Works*, ed. Jerome J. McGann (Oxford: Clarendon Press, 1980–) 1:360–63. The latter work is hereafter referred to as *CPW*.

2. See poems 24, 25, 28, in *CPW* 1.

3. For complete bibliographical details see *Byron's Works: Poetry*, ed. E. H. Coleridge (London: John Murray, 1901–1904) 7:180–84 and T. J. Wise, *Byron: A Bibliography* ... (London: n.p., 1932–33) 1:50–54. The history of the book's publication is discussed in the *CPW*, 2:268–69. The prose quotations below from *Childe Harold's Pilgrimage: A Romaunt* are taken from the first edition, and page numbers are given in the text.

4. For a more detailed discussion of the context and meaning of the poem see *CPW*, 2, and *Fiery Dust*, part 2. The poem is hereafter parenthetically cited as *CHP*, plus canto and stanza numbers.

5. See *Byron's Letters and Journals*, ed. Leslie A. Marchand (Cambridge, Mass.: Harvard University Press. 1973–82) 9:41; hereafter referred to as *BLJ*.

6. See the commentaries to the Oriental Tales in *CPW*, 3.

7. *CPW*, 3:406–415. For an excellent discussion of the political aspects of two of the books of Byron's tales see Peter Manning, "Tales and Politics: *The Corsair, Lara*, and *The White Doe of Rylstone*," in *Byron: Poetry and Politics* ..., ed.

E. A. Stürzl and James Hogg (Salzburg: Institut für Englische Sprache und Literatur, 1981), pp. 204–30.

8. For a discussion of the history of the poem's publication see *Don Juan: A Variorum Edition*, ed. T. G. Steffan and W. W. Pratt (Austin, Tex.: University of Texas Press, 1958) 1:25–52 *passim* (hereafter cited as *DJV*).

9. See *DJV*, 2:3–20 and 4:4–15. The preface is placed at the beginning of the text of *Don Juan* in *DJV* as well as its sequel, the Penguin modernized edition. Leslie A. Marchand's school edition also places it at the poem's beginning. Such a placement is seriously misleading, however, for Byron not only left this preface in an uncompleted state, he discarded it.

10. *Medwin's Conversations of Lord Byron*, ed. Ernest J. Lovell Jr. (Princeton, N.J.: Princeton University Press, 1966), pp. 164–5.

11. Some of Byron's marginal jottings in canto 14 schematize two of the poem's future episodes, including the death of Juan. These marginalia appear on a scrap of MS (not known to the *DJV* editors) now in the Murray archives. The notations occur on a MS carrying a variant version of lines 479–80.

12. Critics have frequently drawn attention to *Don Juan's* parallels with eighteenth-century picaresque novels. See Elizabeth Boyd, *Byron's "Don Juan"* (1945; rpt. New York: Humanities Press, 1958), esp. chaps. 4–7; Andras Horn, *Byron's 'Don Juan' and the 18th Century Novel*, Swiss Studies in English, No. 51. (Bern: Frank Verlag, 1962), and A. B. England, *Byron's Don Juan and Eighteenth Century Literature* (Lewisburg, Pa.: Bucknell University Press, 1975), esp. chap. 3.

13. See *DJV*, I:13–24; Samuel C. Chew, *Byron in England* (London: John Murray, 1924), chap. 4; and J. J. McGann, *Don Juan in Context* (Chicago: University of Chicago Press, 1976), pp. 51–67.

14. See Boyd, *Byron's "Don Juan,"* pp. 148–50 and Nina Diakonova, "The Russian Episode in Byron's 'Don Juan,'" *The Ariel* 3 (1972): 51–57.

15. Byron's critique of the contemporary world of the restoration operates as well in his treatment of "Suwarrow" in the Russian cantos. For a good discussion see Philip W. Martin, *Byron: A Poet Before His Public* (Cambridge: Cambridge University Press, 1982), pp. 213–17.

16. This is Charles Olson's translation of Herakleitos, frag. 23, which appears as the first line of Olson's poem "The Kingfishers."

EDITOR'S BIBLIOGRAPHICAL NOTE

Although his *Social Values and Poetic Acts: A Historical Judgment of Literary Work* (Cambridge: Harvard University Press, 1988) and *Towards a Literature of Knowledge* (Chicago: University of Chicago Press, 1989), with its chapter on "Lord Byron's Twin Opposite of Truth," postdate *The Beauty of Inflections*, it is fair to say, I believe, that this essay is the culmination of McGann's careerlong engagement (since *Fiery Dust* in 1968) with Byron—critically, ideologically, historically, socially, politically, economically, even psychologically (however much this last is not Freudian or Jungian or any other recognizable formulated approach). Two other essays by McGann representing, as he noted in a letter to me of 27 October 1989, "quite a different way of thinking about Byron for [him]" are: "Byron and the Truth in Masquerade" (forthcoming) and "'My Brain Is Feminine': Byron and the Poetry of Deception," in *Byron: Augustan and Romantic*, ed. Andrew Rutherford (New York: St. Martin's, 1990), 26–51. As intriguing as these post-1985 pieces are, and however "different" their ways of "thinking about Byron," *The Beauty of Inflections* is in some sense McGann's "Book of McGann"—or, if that is outrageous, at least the "Book of McGann's Byron." For all the recent critical lumps his four-book project has received—from *The Romantic Ideology* through *The Beauty of Inflections* to the two books cited in the first sentence above—Clifford Siskin, in his probing and astute review of *Social Values* (*Journal of English and Germanic Philology* 89 (1990]: 234–37), is correct about regarding McGann's work as "positioned at the key intersections of contemporary critical debate: history, textuality, social and political action" (p. 237).

There are few if any analogues to this achievement in Byron studies, but I will cite a few pertinent impingements on or extensions of some of the salient points of this essay: on the *Hours of Idleness* poems, Kurt Heinzelman's and Jerome Christensen's essays in this collection; on the tales, Daniel P. Watkins' different, yet complementary *Social Relations in Byron's Eastern Tales* (Rutherford: Fairleigh Dickinson University Press, 1987); on the economics and politics of Byron's relationship to his publishers, Peter Manning's "Tales and Politics: *The Corsair, Lara,* and *The White Doe of Rylstone*," in *Byron: Poetry and Politics*, ed. E. A. Stürzl and J. Hogg (Salzburg: Universität Salzburg Institut für Anglistik und Amerikanistik, 1981), 204–34, and William H. Marshall's *Byron, Shelley, Hunt, and "The Liberal"* (Philadelphia: University of Pennsylvania Press, 1960); and on the political scene in England and on the Continent Malcolm Kelsall's *Byron's Politics* (Sussex and Totowa: Harvester Press and Barnes & Noble, 1987), especially chapter 1, which lays out Byron's "world" in admirable and telling detail (if with significant differences in its analysis of Byron's interrelationship with the events of Europe circa 1788 to 1818–24), chapter 3, entitled "Harold in Italy: The Politics of Classical History," and chapter 6, "There Is No Alternative: *Don Juan*." For whatever it is worth, Kelsall ignores McGann's critical/historical work.

Impinging on McGann's analysis of, broadly speaking, Byron and politics are the following, which describe a recent rising tide of, again broadly speaking, sociopolitical criticism on Byron. By far the best study to date, other than Kelsall's, is Carl Woodring's pioneering and thorough survey, *Politics in English Romantic Poetry* (Cambridge: Harvard University Press, 1970), 148–229, both entirely superseding the older standard studies: Dom N.

Raymond, *The Political Career of Lord Byron* (London: Allen and Unwin, 1924), and Crane Brinton, The *Political Ideas of the English Romanticists* (London: Oxford University Press, 1926), 147–95. Both also generally go beyond most of the essays in Stürzl's and Hogg's *Byron: Poetry and Politics* collection cited in the previous paragraph. Prior to Woodring and Kelsall, certainly the most important contributions to the subject are four essays by David V. Erdman: "Lord Byron and The Genteel Reformers," *PMLA* 56 (1941): 1065–94; "Lord Byron as Rinaldo," *PMLA* 57 (1942): 189–231; "Byron and Revolt in England," *Science and Society* 11 (1947): 234–48; and "Byron and 'the New Force of the People,'" *Keats–Shelley Journal* 11 (1962): 47–64.

To all of the above I would add Carl Lefevre, "Lord Byron's Fiery Convert of Revenge," *Studies in Philology* 49 (1952): 468–87; E. E. Bostetter, "Byron and the Politics of Paradise," *PMLA* 75 (1960), reprinted in his *The Romantic Ventriloquists* (Seattle: University of Washington Press, 1963), 241–301; Michael Robertson, "The Byron of *Don Juan* as Whig Aristocrat," *Texas Studies in Language and Literature* 17 (1976): 709–24; Paul G. Trueblood, ed., *Byron's Political and Cultural Influence in Nineteenth-Century Europe* (Atlantic Highlands, N. J.: Humanities Press, 1981), especially William Ruddick's essay, "Byron and England: The Persistence of Byron's Political Ideas" (although the volume also includes essays on Byron and France, Germany, Greece, Italy, Poland, Portugal, Russia, Spain, Switzerland, and Europe as a whole); Daniel P. Watkins, "Byron and the Politics of Revolution," *Keats–Shelley Journal* 34 (1985): 95–130; and Angus Calder, ed., *Byron and Scotland: Radical or Dandy?* (Totowa, N. J.: Barnes & Noble, 1989), particularly David Craig's "Byron the Radical" and Andrew Noble's "Byron: Radical, Scottish Aristocrat." See also Michael Foot's very different but interesting tour de force, *The Politics of Paradise: A Vindication of Byron* (London: William Collins, 1988), and Christina M. Root's "History as Character: Byron and the Myth of Napoleon," in *History and Myth*, ed. S. C. Behrendt (Detroit: Wayne State University Press, 1990), 149–65.

Finally, McGann's powerful argument that *Don Juan* "is the Book of Byron because he is its hero, because the poem gives the reader a history of 1789–1824 that is set and framed, at all points, in terms of Byron's history," implicitly raises the question of how the letters and journals may, or may not, be regarded as, if not *the* book of Byron, *a* book of Byron. Extraordinarily enough, critical commentary and analysis of them are disappointingly rare. Leslie A. Marchand's introduction to his magnificent edition of the *Letters and Journals* (Cambridge: Harvard University Press, 1973–82), vol. 1, 1–23, is graceful, perspicuous, unabashedly appreciative, and without obtrusive thesis other than remarking on the letters' "healthy and good-humored cynicism combined with a general benevolence toward human frailty" and on the journals' "exuberance" and "clear candour of their statement of what came uppermost to his active mind" (pp. 18, 23). A more provocative reading of the letters and journals—though not particularly focused on Byron's sociopolitical side—is Frederick W. Shilstone's chapter entitled "'Pardon Ye Egotism': The Dialogue between Soul and Self in the Letters, Journals and Conversations" in his *Byron and the Myth of Tradition* (Lincoln: University of Nebraska Press, 1988), an essay I had hoped to include in this volume but was unable to because of its length.

Other interesting if not compelling efforts at analyzing this rather wondrous prose "kaleidoscope" (one of Byron's terms for *Don Juan*, but equally applicable to the letters and journals) are Charles Keith, "Byron's Letters," *Queen's Quarterly* 3 (Winter 1946–47): 468–77; Jacques Barzun, "Introduction: Byron and the Byronic in History," in his *Selected Letters of Lord Byron* (New York: Farrar, Straus, Young, 1953): vii–xii; John D. Jump, "Byron's Prose," in *Byron: A Symposium*, ed. Jump (London: Macmillan, 1975), 16–34, and his "Reflections on Byron's Prose," *The Byron Journal* 3 (1975): 46–56; Nina Diakonova, "Byron's Prose and Byron's Poetry," *Studies in English Literature* 16 (1976): 547–61; and L. J. Findlay, "'Perpetual Activity' in Byron's Prose," *Byron Journal* 12 (1984): 31–47. To these should be added the numerous reviews by eminent Byron scholars of Marchand's 12-volume edition of the letters and journals. Also well worth consulting is *Byron's Bulldog: The Letters of John Cam Hobhouse to Lord Byron*, ed. Peter W. Graham (Columbus: Ohio State University Press, 1984) and the more narrowly focused but nonetheless fascinating "decoding" of some of Byron's correspondence (and that of his closest friends) in Louis Crompton, *Byron and Greek Love: Homophobia in 19th-Century England* (London: Faber; Berkeley: University of California Press, 1985). Important cautions with respect to the complex difficulties in determining when and where the "real" Byron speaks "straight"—particularly in his variously "recorded" conversations—may be found in Ernest J. Lovell's introductions to *His Very Self and Voice: Collected Conversations of Lord Byron* (N. Y.: Macmillan, 1954) ix–xl, and to *Lady Blessington's Conversations of Lord Byron* (Princeton: Princeton University Press, 1969), 3–114.

FRANCES WILSON

Byron, Byronism and Byromaniacs

Will Ladislaw, the motherless and malcontented Childe Harold who wanders through Europe and the Midlands in George Eliot's *Middlemarch*, is asked by Dorothea Brooke whether he would be a poet. 'That depends', he answers,

> To be a poet is to have a soul so quick to discern, that no shade of quality escapes it, and so quick to feel, that discernment is but a hand playing with a finely ordered variety on the chords of emotion—a soul in which knowledge passes instantaneously into feeling, and feeling flashes back as a new organ of knowledge. One may have that condition by fits only.

'"But"', Dorothea replies, '"you leave out the poems."'[1] Ladislaw might well forget that a poet needs poems because the literary scene in 1832, the year in which *Middlemarch* is set, was dominated by the personality and not the poetry of the Romantic hero whose corpse, disfigured by the autopsy of inept doctors, had eight years since been shipped back to England from revolutionary Greece. The death at thirty-six of George Gordon, 6th Lord Byron, had sent shock-waves through Europe, having 'something', Edward Bulwer Lytton said, 'of

From *Byronmania: Portraits of the Artist in Nineteenth- and Twentieth-Century Culture*, edited by Frances Wilson (London: Macmillan Press Ltd., 1999): 1–23. © 1999 by Frances Wilson. Reprinted with permission of Palgrave Macmillan.

the unnatural, of the impossible' about it.² Byron hypnotised his own generation and dominated the next: his life and times (as well as the mysteries of his corpse, a matter in which he resembles Argentina's legendary Evita) continue to be the subject of myth and controversy, as the two-hundred or so biographies of him will testify.

But in the hands of the Victorians, Byron's posthumous renown in England increasingly turned into a feverish anti-Byronism which had less to do with his poetry than his pose, although the two were seen as indistinguishable. After Thomas Carlyle commanded, in 1833, that his contemporaries close their Byron and open their Goethe, volumes of Byron's poetry soon vanished and it was the Byronic pout, like the Cheshire cat's residual grin, which remained fixed in its stead. George Eliot, who published *Middlemarch* when the climate against Byron was at its height in 1872, therefore described her proud misanthrope as resembling the newly fashionable Percy Bysshe Shelley, when Ladislaw was really one of the nineteenth century's many Byronic heroes. Others include Mr Darcy, Heathcliff, and Mr Rochester, all of whom are more famous for their temperament than for any literary talent they might possess, for—like Ladislaw—not one of them ever penned a line.

Byron lent his name to the scornful, despairing, and burdened hero of nineteenth-century literature, but he has also frequently appeared 'undisguised' in novels, films, and plays which claim to give an account of various aspects of his life. Even amongst these biographical fictions however, it is rarely mentioned that Byron wrote at all, not least that he wrote compulsively or that it was the appeal of his poetry and not of his appearance which first caught the eye of the public. Non-biographical narratives likewise feature Byron, and in William Gibson's and Bruce Sterling's 1990 science-fiction novel, *The Difference Engine*, he figures not as a Romantic poet but as a Victorian Prime Minister. One hundred years earlier, in 1891, the criminologist Cesare Lombroso used Byron's personality in his influential study, *The Man of Genius*, as an example of the 'morbid' condition of such men. Lombroso never mentions what Byron might be a genius *of*: the poems are not referred to. Instead, Lombroso turns Byron into a series of pathological symptoms, and he cites the club foot, his childhood love affairs, his intense reaction to seeing Edmund Kean act, his maltreatment of women, and his dislike of the cold as evidence of Byron's hereditary degeneration.

The Victorians invented their own version of Byron against whom they measured their moral progress, and the dissolute figure who Byron was now cast as being became a yardstick for the heroic ideal of the mid- to late nineteenth century. In *Felix Holt* it is remembered that Byron was a poet, but his poetry is seen as one more carnal indulgence. The eponymous radical of George Eliot's 1866 novel picks up a volume of Byron being read by Esther Lyon, 'whose acquaintance with Oriental love was derived chiefly from Byronic poems',[3] and denounces her favourite poet as 'a misanthropic debauchee whose notion of a hero was that he should disorder his stomach and despise mankind'.[4] Austere and impassioned, Felix Holt shares Byron's intensity as well as his politics, but sees in him a rival for Esther's love and not a role model for himself Felix regards the poet as representing only 'lust and pride' and when Esther later accuses him of seeming melancholy, Felix responds that even if he were melancholic he at least would not 'think himself a fine fellow' because of it, in the 'Byronic-bilious style'.[5] The heartbroken Captain Benwick in Jane Austen's *Persuasion* (1818) was proud of his melancholy. He identified with the pain of Byron's heroes, collapsing over 'the impassioned descriptions of hopeless agony' in *The Giaour* and *The Bride of Abydos*, leading Anne Eliot to 'hope he did not always read only poetry' and 'to recommend a larger allowance of prose in his daily study'.[6] In *Nightmare Abbey*, his comic send-up of Byronism written in the same year as *Persuasion*, Thomas Love Peacock has Mr Flosky describe how the cult of melancholia has, like 'that new region of the belles lettres, which I have called the Morbid Anatomy of Black Bile',[7] poisoned the mind of the 'reading public', and Flosky credits Byronism with inspiring the cultish 'gloomy brow' and 'tragical voice'.

In order to understand something of the peculiar violence caught in his shifting reputation and representation, the contributors to this collection of essays on Byron also leave out the poems. They focus instead on the image of the poet and on the phenomenon of 'Byromania', the term first used in 1812 by Annabella Milbanke to describe the contemporary rage for Byron and the Byronic. Annabella did not suffer from Byromania herself, which is probably why she and Byron married three years later, but Lady Byron would later find other terms to describe rage and her husband when she fled their marital home after twelve months, leaving Byron to flee the country, the two of them never to meet again. When Byron returned to England eight years later it was in a coffin and his half-sister, Augusta Leigh—who knew his body better than she should—did not recognise her brother, describing the person lying there as I 'so altered that I could scarcely persuade myself it was he—not a vestige of what he was'. If Byron failed to resemble himself in death, then this was only the continuation of a process begun while he was living: Byron complained that he had became unrecognisable even before being bled lifeless by leeches in Missolonghi, and these essays tell the tale of how he was fed-upon out of all recognition by an entire industry of writers, readers, reviewers, and revengers.

Following the breakdown of his marriage, Byron moved from the centre of society to its margins, from the position of literary lion to that of social outcast. Next to the rapid rise and fall of his reputation, the most remarkable feature of Byron's career is the speed and energy of his development as a poet, and it was in exile that his strongest poetry was produced. While his London-based friends and publisher were censoring Cantos 1 and 2 of 'Lord Byron's last flash poem', as Keats called *Don Juan*, Byron's earliest poetry, written just ten years before, had neither inspired the adulation nor the reproval of his audience. *Hours of Idleness* was published in 1807 when Byron was barely out of his adolescence, and its reception was summoned up in Henry Brougham's review: 'whatever judgement may be passed on the poems of this noble minor, it seems we must take them as we find them, and be content: for they are the last we shall ever have from him'.[8] In response to Brougham's contemptuous criticism Byron brought out, in 1809, the satirical and equally indifferently received *English Bards and Scotch Reviewers*. He then explored Europe and the Levant until 1811. Byromania did not therefore begin until March 10, 1812 and the appearance of the first two cantos of the poem Byron had begun on his travels, *Childe Harold's Pilgrimage*, after which the author, now twenty-four years old, famously awoke to find himself famous and the most celebrated English poet of his—or of any—age.

Childe Harold, said the Duchess of Devonshire when it was first published, 'is on every table, and himself courted, visited, flattered and praised wherever he appears ... he is really the only topic of almost every conversation—the men jealous of him, the women of each other'.[9] The banker-poet, Samuel Rogers, noted that it was Byron's youth and rank, together with his 'romantic wanderings in Greece' which 'combined to make the world stark mad about *Childe Harold*' and its author, for Byron was identified by his readers with his aristocratic and world-weary protagonist.[10] The success of *Childe Harold* was followed, in 1814, with 10,000 copies of *The Corsair* being sold on the day of its publication (Shelley sold almost nothing in his lifetime). By 1815, *Childe Harold* was in its tenth edition and when *Don Juan* Cantos 3, 4 and 5 were published, 'parcels of books were given out of the window' of the premises of Byron's publisher in Albemarle Street, in response to the 'obstreperous demands' of the bookseller's messengers.[11] But it is now forgotten that Byron became the master of *ottava rima* and was Wordsworth's equal in the consistency and sheer quantity of his poetic output: one of the effects of Byromania is that Byron's quality as a poet has been left out of his reputation.

Byron sought to imitate the success of *Childe Harold* by repeating the winning formula of erotic heroes in exotic settings in the poetic tales he poured out over the following few years. Thus *The Giaour*, *The Bride of Abydos*, *The Corsair*, and *Lara* contain what Bertrand Russell called, in his chapter on the Byronic Hero in the *History of Western Philosophy*, the type of the continental 'aristocratic rebel', whose rebellion 'takes the form of titanic, cosmic, self assertion ...'. Meanwhile, others began imitating Byron. It was not only Lady Caroline Lamb who could be found, as Annabella Milbanke described it in 'The Byromania', 'smiling, sighing, o'er his face / In hopes to imitate each strange grimace': the Byronic 'look' was mimicked everywhere by people who 'practised at the glass, in the hope of catching the curl of the upper lip, and the scowl of the brow'.[12] Many of Byron's readers, even 'his passionate admirers', never got beyond what Matthew Arnold later named this 'theatrical Byron, from whom they caught the fashion of deranging their hair or of knotting their neck handkerchief or of leaving their shirt collar unbuttoned'. How many readers, Arnold asked in his attempt to redeem Byron for the Victorians, 'profoundly felt his vital influence, the influence of his splendid and imperishable excellence of sincerity and strength'?[13] Byron's earlier critics held that the appeal of the theatrical Byron would disappear as his death was forgotten and his life was forgiven.

This way room would be left for the 'sincerity and strength' of Byron's poetry to be appreciated on its own merits and flaws and not those of its author. But the reverse would be the case: Byromania was not so fleeting a fad. Even today, when Byron's work is known less well than that of other Romantic poets, more people are conversant with Byronism—the cult inspired by Byron and his heroes—and with the Byronic Romantic 'look', than they are with the appearance and philosophy of Blake or Wordsworth, whose poetry they might know better.

Yet Byron's poetry once had the same impact on his readers as his personality, for another effect of Byromania was the extraordinary and unparalleled counter-culture of imitations which his writing also inspired. In no other area was the unity and authenticity of Byron's identity challenged so much as in the vast array of literary parodies and continuations which surrounded him. 'The bibliographic history of no other modern English poet', Samuel Chew writes, 'contains a chapter similar to this',[14] and the body of 'Byroniana' which has been solidly documented by Chew ranges from the witty mimicry of *Childe Harold* in Horatio and James Smith's 1812 *Rejected Addresses* to the anonymous satire, *Don Leon*, a pornographic hymn to the joys of sodomy printed after Byron's death. This was, along with at least thirty other texts, attributed to Byron himself, who did his best from his exile in Italy to repudiate the claims:

> All the things attributed to me within the last five years—
> Pilgrimages to Jerusalem, Deaths upon Pale Horses, Odes
> to the Land of the Gaul, Adieus to England, Songs to
> Madame La Valette, Odes to St. Helena, Vampires, and
> what not—of which, God knows, I never composed nor
> read a syllable beyond their title in advertisements....[15]

Byron now belonged to his readers, as if by being read the writer were literally purchased. The 'Byronic' became public property and Byron found that his identity was no longer synonymous with his image, that there was a severance between the self he experienced himself as being and the self returned to him in the eyes of his audience. Writing, Byron discovered, 'rather than expressing and preserving the self as it is ... calls the identity of the self (with itself) into question'.[16] 'In this way', Carolyn Steedman writes of her relationship with her mother, but her observation is entirely applicable to Byron, as if he were to his public as a child is to a parent, 'In this way, you come to know that you are not quite yourself, but someone else: someone has paid the price for you and you have to pay it back'.[17] While Byron was identified entirely with the heroes of his poetry and while his imagined presence in the poems was responsible for their tremendous value, the essays in this collection show how that same presence was not necessary in order for the Byronic appeal to be maintained, and Byron had fast to shed himself of any exclusive claim he might feel he had to his representation and his writing. Byron tried hard to control the image of himself being produced but he also identified with it, feeling his reflection to be more finished and complete than the fragmented figure he experienced himself as being.

The onslaught of repetitions and impersonations continued throughout the nineteenth century. In the face of this hall of mirrors, Byron's fight for recognition of his own originality was ironic because the poses and masquerades in both his poetry and social circulations alike mocked the very idea of having an original and unique self to defend. Not only was he famously chameleon, being, he said, 'everything by turns and nothing long', but the layers of Byron's persona were themselves based upon literary imitations. 'Byron did not project life into literature nearly so much as he projected literature into life',[18] Peter L. Thorslev argues in *The Byronic Hero*, and the Byronic was no more the invention of Byron than the Satanic was thought up by Satan himself. The doomed *homme fatal* is the product of bibliogenesis: the Byronic hero can be found in the devilish charms of Milton's fallen angel in *Paradise Lost*, Goethe's *Faust*, Lovelace in Samuel Richardson's *Clarissa*, Valmont in Chanderlos de Laclos' *Les Liaisons Dangereuses*, and the gothic villains of Mrs Radcliffe's bestselling novels. Mario Praz even argues that Byron's reputed sadism towards his wife came not from the twists and turns of his individual psyche but as a result of reading the Marquis de Sade. And Byron was fed back into literature: apart from his appearance as Mr Cypress in *Nightmare Abbey*, who had quarrelled with his wife and was therefore absolved from all duty to his country, Byron appeared as a melancholic character in three other novels during his lifetime.[19] Along with the literary imitations he inspired and the Byronic heroes of his own poetry, the effect of these fictionalisations (which would increase) on Byron was that it became no longer possible for the public to tell the 'original' from the copies made of him. Looking back on an age of Byromania, George Brandes noted in 1905 that a reason for the decline in his reputation was that Byron became damned by association:

> A whole succession of Byron's admirers and imitators have forced themselves inbetween him and us, obscuring the figure, and confusing our impression of the great departed. Their qualities have been imputed to him, and he has been blamed for their faults.[20]

Bulwer Lytton—who enacted his youthful identification with Byron by having an affair with the infamous Lady Caroline Lamb shortly before her death—noted of the poet's other imitators that in their 'whining' weaknesses they precisely missed 'The great characteristics of Lord Byron', which are 'vigour, nerve—the addressing at once the common feelings and earthly passions—never growing mawkish, never girlishly sentimental'.[21]

When the Cambridge Apostles debated the merits of Shelley over Byron at the Oxford Union in 1829, none of the Oxford dons had heard of Shelley and thought that it must be Shenstone who was being defended. But by the mid-nineteenth century Byron's poetic reputation had been overtaken by those of Shelley and Keats, who conformed more to the belief expressed by Walter Bagehot that poetry was not 'a light amusement for idle hours, a metrical species of the sensational novel'—as he considered Byron's racy verses to be— but rather 'a serious and a deep thing'.[22] Thackeray agreed: 'That man *never* wrote from his heart', he cried in his famous and influential attack on Byron,[23] but if Byron's poetry appeared to be not enough in earnest, then this was part of his desired Byronic effect. Byron was the first to demystify his art, to admit—before Thackeray—that he indeed 'got up rapture and enthusiasm with an eye to the public'.[24] He did not want to be seen as a sedentary poet with writer's block, but rather as a man of action who wrote as fast as he lived and with as much nonchalance. Byron, Walter Scott observed in a review of *Childe Harold*, 'manages his pen with the careless and negligent ease of a man of quality'. In other words, Byron posed as an aristocrat even when he wrote, thus distinguishing himself from the despised 'Lakists' and the 'Cockney School', and making Wordsworth, Coleridge and Keats seem bothered and bourgeois in contrast with his own effortless ease and class. Besides writing poems, Byron was producing a certain image of himself as a poet: '*Lara*, I wrote while undressing after coming home from balls and masquerades in the year of revelry, 1814. *The Bride* was written in four, *The Corsair* in ten, days'. But so effective was his posturing that Carlyle, who followed fashion by idolising Byron after his death and demonising him ten years later, asked whether the great poet of the Romantic age had ever, in fact, been anything 'but a huge *sulky Dandy*?'[25] Byronism had displaced Byron altogether.

Carlyle could never decide how he felt about Byron, shifting from seeing him as a 'Power-man; the strongest of his kind in Europe', to 'a sham strong man', but his revision of Byron's significance raises important questions. What *did* Byron represent to his fanatical readers, and why have his many and various guises been reduced to that of a music-hall villain? Why is it that Byron is remembered more for sartorial splendour than for his satirical classic, *Don Juan*; the poem which was praised in the anonymous *Byroniana: Bozzies and Piozzies* in 1825, as being 'the finest example of comic poetry ever produced'? Why is Byronism associated with the gloomy egotism of vampires and not with the quick-fire wit of Byron's writing? *Byromania* is concerned with all these points and the essays which follow give an account not of Byron himself but of his myth, the process by which the figure was drained of his content, leaving only what Lord Macaulay, the earliest Victorian apologist for Byron and Byronism, called 'the magical potency which once belonged to the name of Byron'.[26]

When a name adopts a magical potency it becomes, according to Roland Barthes, a myth. Myths result from a closed and contained word or 'sign', the marriage of a concept and an image, being stripped of its imagined sense of completion and becoming a mere 'signifier', a word without a stable referent or meaning. So in the construction of a myth, the signifier dissociates itself from what it conventionally signifies and refers instead to something entirely separate, to a different and constantly changing set of secondary cultural

associations. The face of Greta Garbo, for example, has become
mythical because its image signifies not the Swedish film actress of the
thirties, but rather, according to Barthes, a 'Platonic Idea of the
human creature'.[27] In the case of Byron, the magical potency' of his
name suggests a certain style and an attitude rather than the historical
figure who lived between 1788 and 1824, wrote poetry, married for a
disastrous year in 1815, fathered two daughters, travelled widely around
Europe and died fighting for Greek independence. Barthes writes that
'there is no fixity in mythical concepts: they can come into being, alter,
disintegrate, disappear completely'.[28] The history of Byron's
mythologisation incorporates all of these stages, and some of them
simultaneously, so that opposing ideas about Byron and the Byronic
were circulating together. Byronism has represented at the same time
both solitary elegance and gross libertinism, physical indulgence and
emaciation; the sharp dandy as well as the dishevelled wanderer are said
to look 'Byronic', and Byron was being erased officially at the same time
as he was being recreated in the subculture of Byroniana.

Not only has Byron been hard to place in the canon of English
literature because he became so quickly the stuff of myth. He also
presents difficulties because for many readers Byron appeals to the
unconscious and to the pleasures of fantasy life before he is read for
literary merit. Byron was a figure of identification and desire in the
public imagination in a way that Southey and Wordsworth simply
were not, and in this sense he became what is now called a celebrity
or 'star', and Byromania can be seen as an early example of fanaticism.
The American poet, Longfellow, noted how Byron invited his
impressionable readers to fantasise that they *were* him, and
Longfellow's analysis of Byromania in America could just easily be
applied to the impact on their public of James Dean or Mick Jagger,
the Byronic heroes of the 1950s and 60s.

> Minds that could not understand his beauties could imitate
> his great and glaring defects ... until at length every city,
> town and village had its little Byron, its self tormenting
> scoffer at morality, its gloomy misanthropist in song.[29]

Christine Gledhill argues that stardom has been achieved by
actors when their 'off-screen life styles and personalities equal or

surpass acting ability in importance'[30] and John Murray, Byron's publisher, found that Byron's poetry could be marketed in much the same way. 'The life of Byron', Arthur Symons observed, 'is a masque in action ... Byron still lives for us with such incomparable vividness because he was a man first and a poet afterwards ...'.[31] In 1821 the *London Magazine* wrote of Byronism that, 'The personal interest, we believe, has always been above the poetical in Lord Byron's compositions; and, what is much worse, they seem to have been, in almost every instance, studiously calculated to produce this effect'.[32] However, the personal interest in Byron, which was growing in response to the rumours of his Gothic background and unconventional private life, did not surpass the poetical so much as become confused with it. Thus when his marriage broke down and, hotly pursued by gossips and bailiffs, Byron bid England farewell, Walter Scott wrote that the poet had 'Childe Harolded himself, and outlawed himself, into too great a resemblance with the pictures of his imagination',[33] suggesting that the public saw Byron's writing as having *written him*, the poetry anticipating and dictating the life of the poet.

Byromania anticipated in other ways the relation of fans to film and media stars. A corollary of the interest in the actor's personality outside his or her work is the fantasy that the stars of a film are playing themselves, that an on-screen affair between the lead players is continued off-screen or that an off-screen affair is imitated on-screen, and that they will continue to play themselves in each new film—that the star's performance and personality are the same thing. Clint Eastwood therefore gives a repeated performance of Clint Eastwood just as Byron was seen as giving a performance of himself in the persons of Childe Harold, Lara, Manfred and Don Juan. Byron colluded with the idea that his work was a continuation of his life and he flirted with his readers, hinting at diabolical deeds in his past, including murder and incest, whilst furiously protesting against any identification which was made between himself and his mysterious characters: 'I by no means intend to identify myself with *Harold* but to *deny* all connection with him.... I would not be such a fellow as I have made my hero for all the world'.[34] Inevitably, in the face of so many secrets and so many clues, unable to discover the truth about Lord Byron from the poet himself, his public looked to his poetry and found him out in the figures such as Lara:

In him inexplicably mix'd appear'd
Much to be loved and hated, sought and feared;
Opinion varying o'er his hidden lot,
In praise or railing ne'er his name forgot:
His silence form'd a theme for others' prate—
They guess'd, they gazed, they fain would know his fate.
What had he been? what was he, thus unknown,
Who walk'd their world, his lineage only known?
A hater of his kind? yet some would say,
With them he could seem gay amidst the gay;
But own'd that smile, if oft observed and near,
Waned in its mirth, and wither'd to a sneer;
That smile might reach his lip, but pass'd not by,
None e're could trace his laughter to his eye....[35]

Victorian anti-Byronism came to see Byron's masquerades in his poetry and public life as a source of contempt. The discourse around him became often concerned with his 'sincerity', and Byron's reputation waned at the same time as his performance of himself was no longer seen to be 'truthful'. When he was eventually spoken of as imitating Byronism, thus imitating imitations of himself, it was not a social or psychological insight which was made, but a moral accusation, a condemnation of character. The representation of Byron as an actor 'strutting about', as Leigh Hunt bitterly said, 'on a stage',[36] was a criticism increasingly levelled against him in the hope that by exposing his artificiality, Byron's mythological status would crumble. But demythification only gives myth greater freedom: the exposure of Byron's inauthenticity fuelled the fascination he held for the public, much as Pamela Anderson's idealised femininity is only perceived as greater in the knowledge that her body is not strictly hers and Diana's non-royal status strengthened her appeal as a princess.

Whilst on the one hand acknowledging that Byron only posed as Byronic, on the other hand his readers saw him as quite genuine: Byron was the sum of his masquerades. Authentification, Richard Dyer argues, is vital in the construction of stardom and the 'true star' has to appear to be the real thing as well as an ideal image.[37] Byron was considered a product of hype and of self-promotion at the same time as he was regarded as natural: a born star. And the ease with which Byron's image could contain this contradictory balance had much to do with his background, which not only sounded like the plot of a gothic novel—'So sad and dark a story is scarcely to be found in any work of fiction', wrote Macaulay[38]—but also conforms to the romantic tales of origins spun by children in their fantasy lives. Freud's essay, 'Family Romances', discusses the daydream commonly had by children that they are adopted and are of higher birth than their parents. The child's nobility must be unthreatened and so the rivalry of siblings is dealt with by the revelation that they are in fact illegitimate, making the dreamer the only heir. An added advantage of this bastardisation is that the child can legitimise any incestuous desires he might have for a brother or sister. Byron's family romance was largely realised, and in this sense the pattern of his life operated uncomfortably closely to the material of unconscious fantasy.[39] Byron was an only child who inherited his uncle's Barony by chance, on the death of the 5th Lord Byron's grandson. He became a peer, and thus his mother's social superior, aged ten. The beautiful Lord Byron moved from Scotland to the ancient Newstead Abbey in Nottingham with the plain Mrs Byron: his glamorous and dissolute father—'mad Jack'—had conveniently died in 1791. A relationship with his half-sister, Augusta, was rumoured—mostly by Byron himself—to have produced a child, Medora.

If one fantasy about stars is that in belonging to another class of person they are not subject to the same experiences as the common breed, simply by introducing himself to his readers as a poet of the aristocracy made Byron stand out as sufficiently different to ignite the public's imagination. Caught between a middle-class Scottish childhood and an ancient English name, Byron could do an imitation of ordinariness as well as of stardom: he was an ordinary man playing the part of an aristocrat as well as an aristocrat playing the part of an ordinary man, and these two images were manipulated by Byron and his readers to great effect.

II

In his remarkable book on the Romantics, the poet and critic Arthur Symons observed that, for

> Most of his life [Byron] was a personality looking out for
> its own formula, and his experiments upon that search
> were precisely the kind to thrill the world. What poet ever
> had so splendid a legend in his lifetime? His whole life was
> lived in the eyes of men, and Byron had enough of the
> actor in him to delight in that version of "all the world's a
> stage."[40]

Together with his awareness of a powerful and influential public
who were busy turning him into a fantasy figure, Byron was a highly
self-conscious performer, and the battle for control of his
representation is the topic pursued in several of these essays. For
Peter W. Graham, Byron was as fascinated as his audience by the art
of Byronic mythmaking, and he was an active participant in perfecting
his own persona. Using his major trope of 'the truth in masquerade',
Byron created, revealed, and dramatised himself through concealment
and disguise, a technique whose many layers and complexities
confound the too-simple reading of his poetry which equates 'this
character' with 'that real person'. Life and performance became for
Byron the same thing—'*What*, after *all*, are *all* things—but a *Show?*—
and Byron's ploy was 'mythmaking that resists or weaves two or more
"things existent" into a fictive whole', blending 'life and art, like jam
swirled into Thomasina's rice pudding in Tom Stoppard's *Arcadia*, so
that distinguishing one from the other becomes impossible'.
Contrasting the dark, melancholy and world-weary Byron of the
youthful *Childe Harold* with the witty, cosmopolitan, urbane Byron of
Don Juan, Graham sees that they in fact have much in common, both
acting as vehicles for fashioning the myth the poet most wanted: that
of mythmaker.

James Soderholm pursues Byron's own formula for dramatising
his 'self-styled legend' by examining the poet's experiments in
fashioning his personality through opaque and oblique—often
diabolical—confessions, whose uncertain relation to the truth only
added to the poet's mystery and thus his appeal. This partial self-
exposure anticipates the 'englamoured rituals of disclosure
characteristic of modern fame, except that Byron is more canny than
his unedited counterparts, who "tell all" in order to make themselves
appear more fascinating'. Byron's idiosyncratic choice of self-display

can be seen most significantly in his teasing of the brother–sister incest theme in his 'most sinuous confession', *Manfred*. Here and elsewhere, Byron's confessions are 'a mode of presentation in which disguise and disclosure intermix and where the aim is not forgiveness or self-expiation, but rather rhetorically evoking various responses in one's audience to manipulate one's own image'.

The theatricality of his confessional rhetoric brings Byron's autobiographical games closer to those of Rousseau than to St Augustine or Wordsworth, for both Byron and Rousseau, 'are without question exhibitionists who oddly combine the confession with the art of violating one's own privacy'. It is not simply Byron's own privacy which is violated in *Manfred*'s strange mixture of candour and duplicity. Consistently implicating his sister in the crime, Byron undermines the sincerity of his confession whilst publicising their risky secret. But this is the point: Soderholm argues that these dark admissions bespeak a desire for exile and for difference, a 'self-assertion vital to the forging of myths and legends'.

Byron's hints in his poetry and letters of possessing a demonic secret are explored in Tom Holland's essay, 'Undead Byron'. Reading the Eastern Tales 'as a meditation upon a type of secret knowledge which at once both ennobles and damns those few men who possess it', Holland traces the rumours of vampirism which surrounded writings by and about Byron and which have never quite been shaken off, so that today the classic figure of the vampire is Byron's blood relation: a dandyish, high-born, anti-hero. For Byron was not only thought to be the author of John Polidori's story, *The Vampyre*, it was also assumed that he was Polidori's subject, and his public attempts to dissociate himself from the tale only lent the rumours credibility: Byron took his association with vampires seriously enough to refute. Tom Holland neatly plays with the ambiguities and silences in Byron's secrets and confessions, showing how they piece together to make a classic vampire tale.

If Byron was a blood-sucking aristocrat, then by seducing his readers he made vampires of them too. The contemporary appetite for Byron was monstrous: metaphors of appetite and consumption, monstrosity and vampirism appear not only in writings by and about Byron but they are similarly employed by Karl Marx. Focusing on this rhetoric in Marx, Byron, and Byromania, Ghislaine McDaytor examines Byron's increasingly uncomfortable involvement with his rapidly multiplying industry. She reads the cult of Byromania alongside its coincidence with the emergence of capitalism and the accompanying 'cultural pressures of literary commodification', which brought a 'dramatic shift in the relations of production ... between the authors, their works and the reading public'. 'Conjuring Byron' traces Byron's growing alienation from his own image and product, his 'shift from poet-producer to slave of industry'. Like Graham above, McDaytor contrasts the image-making of the younger Byron with that of the elder and she argues that while Byron was happy to play with the 'discourse of celebrity that had been constructed around him' in the early years of his fame, this same discourse made the Byron of the 1820s increasingly uncomfortable. For example, Byron's one-time collusion with his reputation as a vampiric seducer—apparent in poems such as *The Giaour* in which he 'pandered' to his poetic construction—shifts in his later years, when he preferred to 'position himself as the victim to vampiric forces'.

So in contrast to Peter W. Graham, James Soderholm, and Tom Holland, who see Byron as complicit to the last in his own mythmaking, Ghislaine McDaytor argues that, 'while Byron's critics may have seen him as actively producing and rigidly controlling his literary image in the public realm, it did not take long for Byron himself to realise his own relative insignificance in the construction of his public image—and its absurdity'. McDaytor examines the importance of the forgeries and imitations which began to reproduce Byron at an astonishing rate after his exile in 1816, and she argues that in the face of this industry of Byroniana, Byron lost control over his representation. For example, it was not Byron himself who provided the model for Polidori's representation of the Satanic milord in his 1819 tale, *The Vampyre*, although Polidori had been Byron's doctor and travelling companion in 1816 and could easily have crafted a story around his impressions of his employer. Instead, Polidori's anti-hero, de Ruthvyn, is based on Lady Caroline Lamb's Lord Ruthven in *Glenarvon*, her own 1816 imitation of her one-time lover. Byron may as well be dead: he had become unnecessary. He had become, McDaytor observes, 'a facsimile of himself'.

Thomas Moore's 1830 *Life* of Byron was treated by its readers not as an biographical account but as 'a sort of authority upon the Art of Being Byronic'.[41] Byron's attempt to control visual reproductions of this art is elegantly explored in Christine Kenyon Jones' essay on Byron's portraits. Kenyon Jones shows how, despite wanting to be seen as 'an unwitting or mainly passive participant in the process' of his own image-making, Byron gave the first contributions to the industry and was absorbed in the art of visual self-presentation. Byron was not only actively involved in the image of himself which appeared in contemporary portraiture—insisting that he be represented as a man of war-like action or as a peer of the realm rather than a poet with a quill—he also went to great lengths to create the emaciated Romantic Byronic 'look' which was identified in his person and in his poetry. Thorwaldsen noted, when sculpting Byron, how the sitter 'was, above all, desirous of looking extremely unhappy'.

Byron's imitation of the Byronic involved rigorous attention to his weight (he tended towards corpulence) and to his deathly-pale pallor, to his clothes and costumes, and to the disguise of his lame foot. In relation to his portraits, Byron has something of Wilde's Dorian Gray about him. Because of his 'very lack of clarity about his own self image', these images exerted power over *him*. They enabled him to 'fix and define his own personality both retrospectively and for the future'—to stabilise himself for himself.

Reviewing Moore's *Life*, Lord Macaulay noted how Byron was 'the mediator between two generations, between two hostile poetical sects'. The Italian Guiseppi Mazzini went further, observing in 1847 that Byron not only 'appears at the close of one epoch, and before the dawn of another', but that he lived 'in the midst of a community based upon an aristocracy which has outlived the vigour of its prime'.[42] Andrew Elfenbein's essay continues this exploration of the divide between the 'aristocratic' Regency and middle-class Victorian England, and the importance for the early-Victorians of fashioning themselves against the perceived immorality of the Regency, which was typified by its adoration of Byron. After his death, Byron and the Byronic were therefore rewritten and Elfenbein draws on Byron's ambiguous role in Benjamin Disraeli's *Venetia* (1837) and in Catherine Gore's *Cecil, or the Adventures of a Coxcomb* (1841), both of which formed part of what was once the hugely popular and is now the forgotten 'Silver-fork' school (see chapter 4). These two novels present a 'Byronised' picture of the Regency period and they place

Byron in a 'symbolic relation' to his time. So if the poet's career manifested a 'flawed brilliance', a 'glittering elegance and moral emptiness' then so too did the Regency age he represented. Disraeli and Gore contrast the superficial, vacuous, homosocial, and aristocratic early-nineteenth-century world in which their novels are set with the stolid Tory values of bourgeois Victorianism. For both writers, the Regency is appealed to in order to be expelled. The formula of these and of numerous other Silver-fork novels was to replace decadent Regency society with 'the sturdy happiness of the bourgeois, companionate marriage', and Elfenbein suggests that the 'inadequacy of Regency values and the need for their ultimate supercession by the supposedly better world of Victorian England' is exposed 'through their treatments of Byron's relations with women'. In both novels, 'part of what seems wrong with the Regency is that the homosocial bonds of male friendship seem stronger than the fragile, transitory relations between men and women'. Silver-fork novels were written for a mass female audience, much as Harlequin and Mills and Boon novellas are today, and the Byronic male's devilish behaviour toward women was the most certain means of getting across the sinful attractions of Byron in order to then reject them—for true sanctity is in the denial of temptation. This way, the new and morally superior epoch could purge its reading public of transgressive Byromania.

The Regency as a time when 'frocks really were frocks and gowns were gowns', and as the symbolic location of the trademark tempestuous Byronic hero is also the recurrent subject of Barbara Cartland's numerous escapist romances (see Chapter 9). Roger Sales argues that Cartland's stereotyped heroes tend to share Byron's biographical details and set about rewriting Byron's life and times, while typically missing the sheer range of the poet's performances and roles. The novels include myths of Byron's family and background, such as sex with servants and orgies at ancient abbeys. The male lead, usually, like Byron, an only child, tends also to be 'cosmopolitan ... well travelled, [and] involved in sexual scandals' while fancying himself a boxer. As with the Silver-fork genre, Cartland's fantasy of the racy and wicked Regency allows her, particularly in the rapidly changing 1960s, to 'engage with very contemporary debates about the permissive society', and her Regency rake is 'at one level celebrated' but 'is also often represented as a dissolute figure who needs to be reformed by the heroine'. For Sales as well as for Elfenbein, the conflict between hero and heroine is class-based and the bourgeois values of the heroine are finally succumbed to by the aristocratic male, who 'gives up his dissolute, permissive, Byronic lifestyle in favour of marriage and life-long romance'. These 'happy' endings rework Byron's own marriage to a reforming woman, a union which ended traumatically because Byron refused to give up his Byronic persona. The comment of the Victorian poet and critic, W. E. Henley, on Lady Byron's choice of husband applies to Barbara Cartland's heroines as well: they should all have married Wordsworth. He, unlike Byron, 'would have had plenty of opportunity to learn "how awful goodness is."'[43]

Aspects of Byron's life were dramatised as early as 1837 in an Italian play by Gian Battista Cipro, *Lord Byron a Venezia*, and the late-twentieth century has seen a flourishing of these Byronic 'bio' dramas, three of which are the subject of Werner Huber's essay. 'Byronic Bioplays' is concerned with the fine line between historical biography and creative literature in the dramatic treatment of Byron's life, and Huber focuses on plays which reveal a post-modern concern with the limits of subjectivity: Howard Brenton's *Bloody Poetry*, Liz Lochhead's *Blood and Ice*, and Tom Stoppard's *Arcadia*. Brenton and Lochhead are more interested in what can be done with narrative itself than they are with historical verisimilitude and temporal linearity, and in this sense their 'life-writing' shows the influence of the 'new' psychological biographies of the twentieth century, of which Virginia Woolf's *Orlando* is an example. Both playwrights present their audience with an entirely different Byron, one who comes closer to the self-conscious Wordsworthian artist-hero than to the paradigmatic Byronic demi-god, and in each play 'aristocratic rebellion is replaced by democratic levelling'. Liz Lochhead's Byron is seen allegorically, as the voice of reason for Mary Shelley as she tries to deal with the series of traumas which characterised her early life. Byron is here the 'counterforce which dialectically engages the optimism and idealism of the Shelleys'. In Brenton's play, Byron emerges as the 'moral centre, the voice of realism and common sense'. Stoppard's Byron is absent throughout, but his life is the focus of admiration, desire and debate; *Arcadia* thus seems at first to reinforce the Byronic legend where *Blood and Ice* and *Bloody Poetry* had debunked it. But Huber argues that Byron's biography and myth function for Stoppard as a 'unifying metaphor for the variety of paradigms alluded to in the play', and the myth of Byron is 'taken to a higher level of abstraction' which is in keeping with the other themes of "lit-math-hort-arch" with which Stoppard is concerned.

The representation of Byron for the twentieth century has been primarily achieved through the cinema, where a version of the Byronic has appeared in the endlessly returned-to figure of Count Dracula, the urbane, aristocratic outsider and seducer of men and women alike. But Byron has appeared under his own name too, and in 'Screening Byron', Ramona Ralston and Sidney Sondergard de-code the semiotics of Byron's appearance in seven films: James Whale's *The Bride of Frankenstein* (1935), David MacDonald's *The Bad Lord Byron* (1948), Robert Bolt's *Lady Caroline Lamb* (1972), Ken Russell's *Gothic* (1986), Gonzalo Suarez's *Rowing with the Wind* (1988), Ivor Passer's *Haunted Summer* and Roger Corman's *Frankenstein Unbound* (1990). What does Byron signify here and to whom is he coded to appeal? For apart from being dressed from one of his portraits and from being cast as handsome, the figure of Byron is markedly different in every film. The famous limp, for example, is sometimes included and sometimes not, is variously on the left foot, the right foot, or both; Ralston and Sondergard show how a historical fact such as Byron's disability operates as 'an open coding that may or may not be employed, depending on the amount of sympathy to be generated for the character; when used it may signify either the cumulative hardships which shaped his personality, or ... his devilish nature'. Further, 'Screening Byron' argues that his cinematic portrait as saint or sinner, poet or idler, radical or reactionary—and he has been all of these—depends on the degree to which those making the film identify with Byron's social position. Byron's cinematic representation is therefore the complicated product of biographical fact, cultural myth, and 'the behind-the-scenes motives and personal idiosyncrasies' of those producing the film.

Peter Cochran, in 'The Life of Byron', is also concerned with Byron's history as a 'cinematic bad guy' and with the way in which Byron's film makers 'appear, in their confused way, to hate him'. By making Byron evil, he is made 'dull—which even his worst enemies rarely accused him of being', and for Cochran the erasure of Byron's celebrated wit is the oddest feature of cinematic Byromania. To the seven films discussed by Ralston and Sondergard, Cochran adds Andy Wilson's bizarre *Dread Poet's Society* (1992) and shows how these eight films form a closed intertextual circuit in which each director draws upon other filmic myths about the life of Byron. Fuseli's painting of 'The Nightmare', for example, which appears in the Villa Diodati of *Gothic* reappears in the Diodati of *Haunted Summer*, Elizabeth Hurley's failed attempt to remove Hugh Grant's boot in *Rowing with the Wind* is similarly borrowed from a scene in Gothic, and in the strangest form of cinematic self-reference the portrayal in *Rowing with the Wind* of Byron's Italian mistress, Margartia Cogni, by the Swedish Bibi Anderson echoes *The Bad Lord Byron*'s representation of Byron's Italian mistress, Teresa Guiccioli, by the Swedish Mai Zetterling, 'Swedes and Italians', Cochran observes, 'being interchangeably improper'. Timothy Spall appears in both *Gothic* and *Dread Poet's Society*, Andy Wilson's film confirming Ralston's and Sondergard's theory above, for *Dread Poet's Society* was co-written by the rap-poet Benjamin Zephania in revenge against Byron's old Cambridge college, Trinity, who offered Zephania a place as Writer in Residence and then rescinded the appointment. Here, as elsewhere, Byron is conjured up in order to signify the film maker's conformity to, or his discontent with, the establishment. Either way, Cochran argues, these films tell us more about the men who made them than they do about Byron.

The fictionalisation of Byron's battles with Lady Caroline Lamb is the subject of my own essay, which considers the representation of Byron's most famous affair as it has been variously described in biography and fiction alike, from Byron's appearance in 1816 in Lamb's own scandalous novel, *Glenarvon*, to the latest biography of Caro published in 1972. Taking their cue from the melodramas of Lamb and Byron themselves, all accounts of their liaison—whether biographical, autobiographical, or fictional; highbrow or middlebrow; pro-Byron or pro-Lamb; Victorian, Edwardian, or contemporary—conform to the classical narrative requirements of the melodrama. In melodrama, character is made subordinate to plot and psychological complexities are reduced to a manichean allegory of good versus evil. In every account of Byron's and Lamb's affair, their complicated exchanges of identity, power, and position are reduced to a skeletal tale of an adult's seduction of a child, and whether it is Lamb or Byron who appears as the seducer or the child depends on whose side the writer is on. For one of the hysterical effects of this traumatic relationship is that it draws everyone in: the critic too becomes melodramatic and seems unable to maintain a neutral position as his or her own fantasies, desires, and fears come into play, and in their treatment of the events they become increasingly voyeuristic, moralising, or paedophilic.

Swinburne hoped that by the year 1900, when the nation stopped to reflect on the 'poetic glories' of the nineteenth century, the name of Byron would be remembered as one of the first. It is the aim of this collection that by the year 2000 we can understand a little more why Byron's name, regardless of his poetic glories, is still one of the first, and that we remember the process by which that name has become so insistently unforgettable. These essays explore something of the strange relation between Byron's identity—on and off the page—and the fantasies of readers, and the identity of readers—on and off the page—and the fantasies of Byron. They tell the tale of how it is that Byron, anticipated by his hero,

> left a Corsair's name to other times,
> Link'd with one virtue and a thousand crimes.

NOTES

1. George Eliot, *Middlemarch* (Harmondsworth: Penguin, 1965), p. 256

2. Edward Bulwer Lytton, *England and the English* (London: Bentley, 1833), vol ii. p, 94.

3. George Eliot, *Felix Holt, The Radical* (Oxford: The World's Classics, 1980), p. 352.

4. Ibid., p. 59.

5. Ibid., p. 219,

6. Jane Austen, *Persuasion* (London: Virago, 1989) p. 100.

7. Thomas Love Peacock, *Nightmare Abbey/Crotchet Castle* (Harmondsworth: Penguin, 1969), p. 69.

8 Henry P. Brougham, unsigned review of *Hours of Idleness*, *Edinburgh Review*, January 1808, in Andrew Rutherford, ed. *Byron: The Critical Heritage* (London: Routledge and Kegan Paul, 1970), p. 32.

9. Vere Foster, *The Two Duchesses: Family Correspondence* (London: Blackie, 1898), p. 376.

10. Samuel Rogers, *Table Talk* (New York: Appleton, 1856), p. 229.

11. Samuel Smiles, A *Publisher and his Friends* (London: John Murray, 1891), I, p. 413.

12. Lord Macaulay, Review of *Thomas Moore's Letters and Journals of Lord Byron: with Notices of his Life* (1830), *Edinburgh Review*, June 1831. Reprinted in Rutherford, p. 316.

13. Rutherford, p. 458.

14. Samuel Chew, *Byron in England* (London: John Murray, 1924), p. 193.

15. Byron, 'Reply to Blackwood's Edinburgh Magazine', *Byron's Letters and Journals*, ed. Leslie Marchand (London: John Murray, 1973) vol. iv, p. 474.

16. Sonia Hofkosh, 'The Writer's Ravishment: Women and the Romantic Author—The Example of Byron', in Anne Mellor, ed. *Romanticism and Feminism* (Bloomington: Indiana, 1988), p. 98.

17. Carolyn Steedman, *Landscape for a Good Woman: A Story of Two Lives* (London: Virago, 1986), p. 105.

18. Peter L. Thorslev Jr., *The Byronic Hero: Types and Prototypes* (Minneapolis: University of Minnesota Press), p. 12.

19. For a list of the fictions in which Byron appeared in his lifetime and posthumously, see the Appendix at the back of the volume.

20. George Brandes, *Main Currents in Nineteenth Century Literature* (New York, Boni and Liveright, 1923), vol. iv. p. 253.

21. Edward Bulwer Lytton, 'Conversation with an Ambitious Student in ill health', *The New Monthly Magazine*, December 1830, quoted in Chew, p, 241.

22. Walter Bagehot, 'Wordsworth, Tennyson, and Browning: or Pure, Ornate, and Grotesque Art in English Poetry', *National Review*, November 1864. Re-printed in Rutherford, p. 366.

23. William Thackeray, *Notes of a Journey from Cornhill to Grand Cairo*, quoted in Chew, p. 256.

24. Ibid.

25. Thomas Carlyle, extract of a letter of 28 April 1832 to Macvey Napier, editor of the *Edinburgh Review*. Quoted in Rutherford, p. 291.

26. Macaulay, *Review*, Rutherford, p. 316.

27. Roland Barthes, 'The Face of Garbo', *Mythologies* (London: Paladin, 1973), p. 56.

28. Barthes, 'Myth Today', *Mythologies*, p. 120.

29. Rutherford, p. 18.

30. Christine Gledhill, ed. *Stardom: Industry of Desire* (London: BFI, 1990), p. xvi.

31. Arthur Symonds, *The Romantic Movement in English Poetry* (London: Constable, 1909), p. 239.

32. Quoted in Rutherford, p. 13.

33. J.G. Lockhart, *The Life of Sir Walter Scott* (Boston: J. B. Millett Co, 1902), vol. v, p. 127.

34. *Byron's Letters and Journals*, vol. 2, p. 122.

35. Byron, *Lara*, Canto I, xvii 289–302.

36. T.W. Reid, *The Life of Lord Houghton*, quoted in Chew, p. 135.

37. See Richard Dyer, 'A Star is Born', in Gledhill, *Stardom: Industry of Desire*, for a discussion of the importance of authentification.

38. Rutherford, p. 296.

39. See my own essay in this collection, 'The Melodramas of Lady Caroline Lamb', for a discussion of the role of the Family Romance in fictions of Byron's childhood.

40. Symons, p. 239.

41. W.E. McCann, 'Byronism', *The Galaxy Miscellany*, June 1868, quoted in Chew, p. 247.

42. Guisseppi Mazzini, 'Byron and Goethe', quoted in Chew, p. 239.

43. Chew, p. 21.

Chronology

1788	George Gordon Byron is born, January 22, in London, to Captain John ("Mad Jack") Byron and Catherine Gordon Byron of Gight.
1790	Catherine Byron, her fortune spent by her husband upon lavish living, takes her son to Aberdeen.
1791	Captain Byron dies at thirty-six in France.
1792	George Gordon attends day school in Aberdeen.
1798	Inherits the title of his great-uncle, the fifth Lord Byron (the "Wicked Lord"), and moves to Newstead Abbey, Nottinghamshire, the Byron family seat.
1798–99	Tutored in Nottingham; clubfoot treated by a quack doctor. Byron is sexually abused by May Gray, the family's Scottish maid.
1799–1801	Attends boarding school at Dulwich, near London.
1801–05	Attends Harrow School and spends his vacations with his mother at Southwell.
1803	First romance with Mary Chaworth of Annesley Hall, grandniece of Lord Chaworth, who had been killed by the "Wicked Lord" in a duel.
1804	Begins correspondence with his half-sister, Augusta.
1805	Enters Trinity College, Cambridge.
1806	*Fugitive Pieces*, first poems, privately printed.
1807	*Hours of Idleness* published. Byron is drawn into a Cambridge circle of young intellectuals and political liberals.

1808	*Hours of Idleness* attacked in the *Edinburgh Review*. Byron receives master's degree at Cambridge in July and moves to London, fully engaged in a life of sensuality.
1809	Takes seat in the House of Lords, March 13. Publishes *English Bards and Scotch Reviewers* in retaliation against the *Edinburgh Review*. With John Cam Hobhouse, he departs in July for a journey through Portugal, Spain, Albania, and Greece. Completes first canto of *Childe Harold's Pilgrimage* in Athens.
1810	Finishes second canto of *Child Harold*, March 28. Travels in Turkey and Greece. Swims Hellespont, May 3. Lives in Athens.
1811	Returns to England in July. His mother dies in August.
1812	Gives three liberal speeches in the House of Lords. *Childe Harold*, published in March, brings immediate fame, and Byron becomes the darling of London's fashionable women. Has affair with Lady Caroline Lamb.
1813	Begins affair in June with his half-sister Augusta Leigh. Publishes first Oriental tales, *The Giaour* and *The Bride of Abydos*.
1814	Publishes *The Corsair* and *Lara*. Daughter Elizabeth Medora born to Augusta in April. Becomes engaged in September to Annabella Milbanke.
1815	Marries Annabella Milbanke, January 12. Hounded by creditors, he flies into frequent rages. Daughter, Augusta Ada, born December 10.
1816	Lady Byron leaves Byron, January 15; formal separation signed on April 21. On April 25, Byron leaves England forever. Spends summer in Switzerland with Shelley, Mary Godwin, and Claire Clairmont, with whom he has an affair. Publishes Canto III of *Childe Harold* and *The Prisoner of Chillon*. Begins *Manfred*. Travels to Italy.
1817	Allegra, daughter by Clair Clairmont, born January 12. Byron resides in Venice and engages in a liaison

with Marianna Segati. Visits Florence and Rome; completes *Manfred* and works on fourth canto of *Childe Harold*; experiments in *Beppo* with colloquial *ottava rima* on the theme of Venetian life.

1818   Begins liaison with Margarita Cogni; abandons himself to dissipation in Venice without losing literary energy. *Beppo* published in February. *Childe Harold*, Canto IV, published in April. Begins *Don Juan*; finishes Canto I in September.

1819   Meets Teresa, Countess Guiccioli, in April, his last liaison. Spends fall with Teresa at La Mira and continues *Don Juan*; the affair is countenanced by her husband. Thomas Moore visits Byron and is given the gift of Byron's memoirs. *Don Juan*, Cantos I and II, published in July.

1820   Byron lives in Guiccioli palace in Ravenna. Continues *Don Juan*; writes first of poetic dramas, *Marino Faliero*.

1821   *Don Juan*, Cantos III, IV, and V, published in August, and Byron promises Teresa not to continue *Don Juan*. In September writes *The Vision of Judgment*. Joins Gambas and Shelley in Pisa in November. *Cain* published in December.

1822   British outcry against *Cain* and *Don Juan* increases. Teresa consenting, Byron resumes *Don Juan*. Shelley drowns in the Bay of Lerici. Byron joins exiled Gambas in Genoa. *The Vision of Judgment* published in October; British outcry excessive. Byron changes to John Hunt as publisher.

1823   London Greek Committee enlists Byron's aid on behalf of Greece. Byron sails in July for Greece; becomes severely ill after strenuous excursion to Ithaca. Sets sail for Missolonghi on December 30. *Don Juan*, Cantos VI through XIV, published.

1824   Hailed in Missolonghi on January 4 as a deliverer. On January 22 writes "On This Day I Complete My Thirty-Sixth Year." Cantos XV and XVI of *Don Juan* published in March. Becomes gravely ill on April 9; incompetent doctors insist on repeated bleedings; dies on April 19. Mourned by Greeks as a national hero. Regarded throughout Europe as "the Trumpet Voice of Liberty," Byron is buried July 16 in Hucknall Torkard Church near Newstead.

Works by Lord Byron

Fugitive Pieces, 1806.

Hours of Idleness, 1807.

Poems Original and Translated, 1808.

English Bards and Scotch Reviewers, 1809.

The Curse of Minerva, 1812.

Childe Harold's Pilgrimage, Cantos i, ii, 1812; iii, 1816; iv, 1818.

The Waltz, 1813.

The Giaour, 1813.

The Bride of Abydos, 1813.

Ode to Napoleon Buonaparte, 1814.

The Corsair, 1814.

Lara, 1814.

Hebrew Melodies, 1815.

The Siege of Corinth and Parisinam, 1816.

The Prisoner of Chillon, 1816.

Manfred, 1817.

The Lament of Tasso, 1817.

Monody on the Death of the Right Hon. R.B. Sheridan, 1817.

Beppo, 1818.

Mazeppa, 1819.

Don Juan, Cantos i., ii, 1819; iii., iv., v., 1821; vi., vii., viii., 1823; ix.,
    x., xi., xii., xiii, xiv, 1823; xv, xvi, 1824.

*A Letter to John Murray on the Rev. W. L. Bowles's Striotures on the Life
    and Writings of Pope*, 1821.

Marino Faliero, and The Prophecy of Dante, 1821.

Sardanapalus, The Two Foscari, and Cain, 1821.

Werner, 1822.

The Vision of Judgment, 1822.

Heaven and Earth, 1822.

The Island, 1823.

The Age of Bronze, 1823.

Canto i. of the *Morgante Maggiore di Messer Luigi Pulci*, translated:
    *A Reading of English Romantic Poetry. The Deformed Transformed,
    1824.*

Parliamentary Speeches in 1812 and 1813, 1824.

Works about Lord Byron

Barton, Anne. *Byron: Don Juan*. Cambridge: Cambridge University Press, 1992.

Blackstone, Bernard. *Byron: A Survey*. London: Longman Group Ltd., 1975.

Bloom, Harold. *The Visionary Company*. Rev. ed. Ithaca: Cornell University Press, 1971.

De Almeida, Hermione. *Byron and Joyce through Homer: "Don Juan" and "Ulysses."* New York: Columbia University Press, 1981.

Drinkwater, John. *The Pilgrim of Eternity: Byron—A Conflict*. New York: George H. Doran, 1925.

Elledge, W. Paul. *Byron and the Dynamics of Metaphor*. Nashville: Vanderbilt University Press, 1968.

Elwin, Malcolm. *Lord Byron's Wife*. Harcourt, Brace & World, 1963.

Foot, Michael. *The Politics of Paradise: A Vindication of Byron*. New York: Harper & Row, 1988.

Franklin, Caroline. *Byron's Heroines*. Oxford: Clarendon Press, 1992.

Frye, Northrup. *Fables of Identity: Studies in Poetic Mythology*. New York: Harcourt, Brace & World, Inc., 1963.

Gleckner, Robert F. "From Selfish Spleen to Equanimity: Byron's Satires." *Studies in Romanticism* 18 (1979): 173–205.

Highet, Gilbert, "The Poet and His Vulture." *Byron: A Collection of Critical Essays*. Paul West, ed. Englewood Cliffs, N.J.: Prentice-Hall, 1963.

Jordan, Frank, ed. *The English Romantic Poets: A Review of Research and Criticism*. 4th ed. New York: MLA, 1985.

Jump, John D., *Byron*. London and Boston: Routledge & Kegan Paul, Ltd., 1972.

Kelsall, Malcolm. *Byron's Politics*. Brighton: Harvester Press, 1987.

Knight, G. Wilson. *Byron and Shakespeare*. New York: Barnes & Nobles, 1966.

———. *Lord Byron: Christian Virtues*. London: Routledge & Kegan Paul, Ltd., 1952.

Longford, Elizabeth. *The Life of Byron*. Boston: Little, Brown, 1976.

Manning, Peter. *Byron and His Fictions*. Detroit: Wayne State University Press, 1978.

———. "Don Juan and Byron's Imperceptiveness to the English World." *Studies in Romanticism* 18 (1979): 207–33.

Marchand, Leslie A. *Byron: A Biography*. 3 vols. New York: Alfred A. Knopf, Inc., 1957.

———. *Byron's Poetry: A Critical Introduction*. Cambridge: Cambridge University Press, 1968.

Maurois, Andre. *Byron*. Hamish Miles, trans., New York: D. Appleton-Century Co., 1930.

McConnell, Frank D., ed. *Byron's Poetry*. New York: W.W. Norton and Company, 1978.

McGann, Jerome J., ed. *Byron*. Oxford: Oxford University Press, 1986.

———. *The Beauty of Inflections: Literary Investigations in Historical Method and Theory*. Oxford: Press, 1985.

———. *"Don Juan" in Context*. Chicago: University of Chicago Press, 1976.

———. *Fiery Dust: Byron's Poetic Development*. Chicago: University of Chicago Press, 1968.

Moore, Doris Langley. *Lord Byron: Accounts Rendered*. London: John Murray, 1974.

Quennell, Peter. *Byron: The Years of Fame, and Byron in Italy*. London: Faber and Faber, 1935.

Robinson, Charles E., ed., *Lord Byron and His Contemporaries: Essays from the Sixth International Byron Seminar*. Newark: University of Delaware Press, 1982.

Rutherford, Andrew. *Byron: The Critical Heritage*. New York: Barnes & Noble, 1970.

———. *Byron: A Critical Study*. Stanford: Stanford University Press, 1961.

Strickland, Margot. *The Byron Women*. New York: St. Martin's Press, 1974.

Stürzl, Erwin A., and James Hogg, eds. *Byron: Poetry and Politics*. Salzburg, Austria: Institut für Anglistik und Amerikanistik, 1980.

Trueblood, Paul G. *The Flowering of Byron's Genius*. Stanford: Stanford University Press, 1945.

Untermeyer, Louis. *Lives of the Poets: The Story of One Thousand Years of English and American Poetry*. New York: Simon and Schuster, 1959.

Vassallo, Peter. *Byron: The Italian Literary Influence*. New York: St. Martin's Press, Inc., 1984.

Wain, John, "The Search for Identity." *Byron: A Collection of Critical Essays*. Paul West, ed. Englewood Cliffs, N.J.: Prentice-Hall, 1963.

West, Paul, ed. *Byron and the Spoiler's Art*. London: Chatto & Windus, Ltd., 1960.

Woodring, Carl. "Nature, Art, Reason, and Imagination in Childe Harold." *Romantic and Victorian: Studies in Memory of William H. Marshall*, W.P. Elledge and R.L. Hoffman, eds. Rutherford: Fairleigh Dickinson University Press, 1971.

WEBSITES

Lord Byron: A Comprehensive History of His Life and Work
http://www.englishhistory.net/byron.html

The Lord Byron Home Page
http://www.lordbyron.ds4a.com/

Selected Poetry of George Gordon Lord Byron
http://eir.library.utoronto.ca/rpo/display/poet45.html

Lord George Gordon Byron
http://www.online-literature.com/byron/

Contributors

HAROLD BLOOM is Sterling Professor of the Humanities at Yale University and Henry W. and Albert A. Berg Professor of English at the New York University Graduate School. He is the author of over 20 books, including *Shelley's Mythmaking* (1959), *The Visionary Company* (1961), *Blake's Apocalypse* (1963), *Yeats* (1970), *A Map of Misreading* (1975), *Kabbalah and Criticism* (1975), *Agon: Toward a Theory of Revisionism* (1982), *The American Religion* (1992), *The Western Canon* (1994), and *Omens of Millennium: The Gnosis of Angels, Dreams, and Resurrection* (1996). *The Anxiety of Influence* (1973) sets forth Professor Bloom's provocative theory of the literary relationships between the great writers and their predecessors. His most recent books include *Shakespeare: The Invention of the Human* (1998), a 1998 National Book Award finalist, *How to Read and Why* (2000), *Genius: A Mosaic of One Hundred Exemplary Creative Minds* (2002) and *Hamlet: Poem Unlimited* (2003). In 1999, Professor Bloom received the prestigious American Academy of Arts and Letters Gold Medal for Criticism, and in 2002 he received the Catalonia International Prize.

KAREN WILLS is the author of two books and numerous articles and short stories for children and adults. Before becoming a full-time writer she practiced law and taught on the college level. Her two grown children are Ian and Beth Swanson.

DUKE PESTA is Assistant Professor of English at Oklahoma State University. He teaches courses in Shakespeare and Renaissance literature, the Bible, and Russian literature.

The late ROBERT F. GLECKNER was Professor Emeritus at Duke University. He was the author of several books on William Blake, Lord Byron, and other romantic poets and authors, including *Byron and the Ruins of Paradise* (1967) and *Critical Essays on Lord Byron* (1991).

JEROME J. MCGANN is the John Stewart Bryan University Professor at the University of Virginia. He has also been the Director of the Victorian Centre, Royal Holloway Cottage at the University of London. His recent publications include *Byron and Romanticism* (2002), *Byron and Wordsworth* (1999), and *Dante Gabriel Rossetti and the Game That Must Be Lost* (2000).

FRANCES WILSON teaches in the School of English and American Literature at The University of Reading, United Kingdom. She is the author of *Literary Seductions: Compulsive Writers and Diverted Readers* (1999) and the editor of *Byromania: Portraits of the Artist in Nineteenth- and Twentieth-Century Culture* (1998).

INDEX

Aberdeen Grammar School, 5, 9
Aeneid, (Virgil), 72
"All is Vanity," 90
Allegra
  attending convent, 50
  daughter of, 46
  death of, 50
Annabella, 36, 65, 68, 135
  journal on Byron, 33–34
  her marriage to Byron, 39–40, 69
  poor treatment of, 39–42
  separation from Byron, 42–43, 73
Arcadia, (Stoppard), 144, 149
Ariosto's tomb, 78
Arnold, Matthew, 135
Augusta, 36, 40–41, 57, 60, 68, 134
  affair with Byron, 65
  burning of Byron's memoirs, 57
  Byron's journal for her, 76
  half-sister of Byron, 15
  her pregnancy, 37
Augusta Ada, 73
  daughter of Byron, 41
Austen, Jane, 133

Bad Lord Byron, The, (film),
    MacDonald, 150–151
Becher, J. T., 61–62
Beppo, 47, 80
  on love triangle, 79
Blood and Ice, (Lochhead), 149

Bloody Poetry, (Brenton), 149
Bloom, Harold, 81–82
  introduction, 1–3
Bolt, Robert, 150
Brando, Marlon, 62
Brenton, Howard, 149
Bride of Abydos, 94, 110, 133, 135
  theme of, 37
Bride of Frankenstein, The, (film),
    Whale, 150
Bridges, Robert, 85
Byromania, 136, 146
  and fanaticism, 140
Byron, Catherine, (mother), 7, 61
  her death, 29
  devotion to Byron, 8
  her romance with Lord Grey, 15
  son's troubles, 20
Byron, John, (father), 6–8, 61
Byron, Lord
  his affairs, 32, 60, 79, 82
  aristocrat, 143
  cinema representation, 150
  his clubfoot, 7–8, 18, 61
  as commander-in-chief, 55
  death of, 57, 83, 131, 134
  his depression, 22
  early years and family, 6–9
  eccentric life of, 47
  fame of, 63
  financial troubles, 19, 22, 29, 35
  on immortality, 91–93

incest, 36, 42, 43, 65
influence of Greece, 27, 51–53
lyric poetry, 85
mythmaker, 144
ordinary man, 143
ostracized, 43–44
poetry as his life, 141
and political influences, 9–10
product of hype, 142
satirical poetry, 79
and self-exile, 119
his style, 62
his title, 5
vampirism, 145
Byron, William, 6
Byronic Bioplays', (essay), Huber, 149
Byronic Hero, 61–62, 64, 71, 75–76,
   79, 135,
   conflicted hero, 77
   fall of, 72–73
   inner man, 71–72
   myth of, 83
   and vulnerability, 68
"Byron's Lyrics," (lecture), Martin, 85

"Cain," 49, 83
Cambridge University, 13, 18, 30, 61
   Byron's life here, 19
   Byron's return to, 21
Candide, 80–81
Carbonari, 49, 82
Cartland, Barbara, 148–149
Cecil, (Gore), 147
Chateau of Chillon
   Byron's tour of dungeons, 75
Chaworth, Mary Ann, 14–15, 23, 45,
   60
   on Byron's affections, 21
Chew, Samuel, 136
Childe Harold's Pilgrimage, 12, 27, 47,
   65, 75, 108, 112

Byron's concerns of, 29
on diary-like quality, 63
fame of, 134–135
freedom, 110
good and evil, 83
Greece, 110–111
on Hobhouse's reaction to, 28
loss, 89
lyricism, 96
as poetic journal, 62
publication of, 31, 63
renewal in the West, 109–110
turning point, 95
"Christabel," (Coleridge), 70
Clairmont, Claire, 44–45, 74
Clarissa, (Richardson), 137
Claughton, Thomas, 35
Clubbe, John, 71
Coat of Arms, 10
Cochran, Peter, 150–151
Conrad, Joseph, 67
Constantinople, 28
Corman, Roger, 150
Corsair The, 37, 67, 101, 135,
   as bestseller, 37
   "orientalist" poetry, 65–66
   similarities between Byron and
      Conrad, 66
"Curse of Minerva, The," 29

Dallas, Robert Charles, 24
Dead Poet's Society, (film), Wilson, 157
Dean, James, 62
de Castelnau, Marquis, 122–123
de Richelieu, Duc, 122
de Ruthyn, 14
de Selincourt, Ernest, 85
de Stael, Madame, 35
Detached Thoughts, 17, 92
Difference Engine, The,
   (Gibson/Sterling), 132
Disraeli, Benjamin, 147–148

Doctor Faustus, (Marlowe), 76
Doctor Glennie's Academy, 11
"Don Juan," 6, 47, 51, 79, 82, 97, 113,
   134–135
  Book of Byron, 118, 124
  constraints on, 113
  as greatest work, 80
  historical repetition, 119
  hope in, 120
  mock epic, 81
  nihilistic, 120
  plot, 115–116
  preface, 114–116
  similar to Byron's life, 120
  on social and political, 121
  structural change, 114
Donne, John, 62
"Dream, The," 45
Drinkwater, John, 8, 13, 31
  and Byron's title, 10
Drury, Joseph, 16
  on Byron's mind, 14
  and headmaster, 12
  his retirement, 16
Drury Lane Theatre, 35, 41
Duchess of Devonshire, The, 31
Duff, Mary
  cousin of Byron, 9
Dunciad, The, (Pope), 80
Dyer, Richard, 142

Eastwood, Clint, 141
Edinburgh Review, 22, 62, 94, 107
Edleston, 19, 21, 30
Elfenbein, Andrew, 147–149
Elgin, Lord, 27, 29
Eliot, George, 131–132
"End of the World, The,"
  (MacLeish), 96
English Bards and Scotch Reviewers, 22,
  23, 62, 134

as counter-attack, 108–109
  human life, 109
  on revising, 23–24
"Epistle to Augusta," 45
*Essai pur l'Histoire Ancienne et moderne
  de la nouvelle Russie*, 122
"Euthanasia," 100

Family Romances, (essay), Freud, 142
"Fare Thee Well," 42
Faust, (Goethe), 45, 137
Fielding, Henry, 80
Frankenstein, (Godwin), 45, 74
Frankenstein Unbound, (film), Corman,
  150
French Revolution, 25
Freud, 142–143
Frye, Northrop, 85–86
Fugitive Pieces, 21, 61, 107

Garrod, H. W., 90
Giaour, The, 28, 35, 110, 133
  on modern Greece, 112
Gibraltar, 26
Gibson, William, 132
"Girl of Cadiz, The," 26
Gleckner, Robert F.
  biographical info, 103–106
  Hebrew Melodies and other Lyrics
    of 1814–1816, 85–106
Glenarvon, (Lamb), 33, 45, 151
Glenhill, Christine, 140–141
Godwin, Mary, 44–45, 74
Goeth, J. W., 76
Gore, Catherine, 147–148
Gothic, (film), Russell, 150–151
Graham, Peter W. 144, 146
Gray, May, 9, 61
Guiccioli, Countess Theresa, 48,
  51–52, 151

Hampton Club, 34
Hanson, John, 9–10, 12, 19, 24, 29,
    144
  on Byron's money problems, 20
  as family lawyer, 9
  finding a school for Byron, 11
"Harp the Monarch Minstrel Swept,"
    (hymn), 87
Haunted Summer, (film), Passer,
    150–151
Heart of Darkness, (Conrad), 67
Hebrew Melodies, 69, 86, 91, 97
  death, 100
  hymns of doom,90, 94
  lyric poetry, 91
  Old Testament, 40
Henry VIII, 6
Hercules, (ship), 52, 83
Highet, Gilbert, 12
"Hints from Horace," 29, 108
History of Western Philosophy, (Russell),
    135
Hobhouse, John Cam, 21, 29, 68–69
  Byron's best man, 38
  and corpse of Byron, 60
  his diary, 38–39
  his traveling, 25–26, 28, 46, 76
Hodgson, Francis
  his friendship with Byron, 21–22
Holland, Tom, 145–146
Hours of Idleness, 21, 62, 93, 107, 135
  attack on, 108
  bad reviews, 22
  distribution of, 22
  first published work, 107
  lyrics in, 94
House of Lords, 30–31
Huber, Werner, 149–150
Hunt, John, 113, 115
Hunt, Leigh, 35, 82, 86, 142
Hydra, (ship), 29
Hyperion, (Keats), 81

Incest, 36, 65, 73, 141
Islam, 111–112

Jack, Ian, 13
Jane Eyre, (Brontë),62
"Jephtha's Daughter," 89–90
Jones, Christine Kenyon, 147

Keats, John, 81, 85, 57, 130, 134
"Kubla Khan," (Coleridge), 70

Lady Caroline Lamb, (film), Bolt, 150
Lamb, Caroline, 31, 34–35, 151, 60
  her affair with Byron, 65, 151–152
  trip to Ireland, 32–33
"Lament of Tasso, The," 78
  turning point in Byron's career, 79
Laura, 135
Les Liaisons Dangereuses, (de Laclos),
    137
Levantine politics, 112
Liberal, The, 50, 82–83
Life, (Moore), 146–147
Life of Byron, The, (Cochran), 150–151
"Lines Inscribed upon a Cup Formed
    from a Skull," 23
Lisbon, 25
Lochhead, Liz, 149
Lombroso, Cesare, 132
London Greek Committee, 83
London Magazine
  on Byronism, 141
Long, Edward, 19
  his drowning, 23
Lord Byron a Venezia, (play), Cipro,
    149

Mac Donald, David, 150
MacLeish, Archibald, 96

"Maid of Athens, The," 28
Man of Genius, The," (Lombroso), 132
"Manfred," 45, 47, 76, 103
  Byron's confessions, 145
  the dark side, 76
Marchand, Leslie, 36
Marlowe, Christopher, 76
Martin, L.C., 85–86
Maurois, André, 17, 29, 31
McDaytor, Chislaine, 145–146
McGann, Jerome J.
  biographical info, 127–130
  The Book of Byron and the Book
    of a World, 107–130
Medora, 40, 68, 143
  daughter of Byron, 37
Medwin, Thomas, 33
Melbourne, Lady, 33–36
  her death, 47
Middlemarch, (Eliot), 131–132
Milton, John, 59, 73
Moore, Thomas, 30, 48, 51, 94, 100
  146–147
  letter from Byron, 63
  possesion of Byron's memoirs, 57
Murray, John, 113–114, 116, 121, 141
  and publisher, 48
"My Soul is Dark," 70, 94

Napoleon, 43, 46, 72, 75, 104, 119
  compared to Byronic Hero, 71
Napoleonic Wars, 25
"Napoleon's Farewell," 72
Nathan, Issac, 69–70
Newstead, 6, 10, 22–24, 29–30
  Byron's estate, 5
  selling of, 35, 41, 52, 79
Nightmare Abbey, (Peacock), 133, 137

Objects of Love, 31–37
"Ode to Napoleon," 72, 101–102

"On this Day I Complete My Thirty-
  Sixth Year," 54
"Orientalist" Poetry, 66
Orlando, (Woolf), 149
"Ozymandias," (Shelley), 70, 72

Paradise Lost, (Milton), 59, 73, 137
"Parisina"
  and incest, 40
Parker, Margaret
  death of, 13
Pasha, Ali, 26–27
Passer, Ivor, 150
Peacock, Thomas Love, 133
Persuasion, (Austen), 133
Pesta, Duke
  biographical info, 84
  Byron and the Romantic Anti-
    Hero, 59–84
Pigot, Elizabeth, 15, 17–18
  offer to copy Byron's poetry, 20
Poems on Various Occasions
  revised, 21
Polidori, John William, 44–45,
  145–146
Pope, Alexander, 80
Portugal, 25
Prisoner of Chillon, The, 45, 75
  on nature, 88
"Prometheus," (Shelley), 74–75, 81
  defeat, 101

Ralston, 150
Rape of the Lock, The, 80
Read, Herbert, 86
Recluse, (Wordsworth), 81
Richardson, Samuel, 137
Ridenour, George, 82
Rogers, Samuel, 30, 135
Rowing with the Wind, (film), Suarez,
  150–151

Russell, Bertrand, 135
Russell, Ken, 150
Russo-Turkish War, 117

"Sailing to Byzantium," (Yeats), 72
Sales, Roger, 148–149
Sardanapalus, 83
"Saul," 89
Scott, Jane Elizabeth, 34
Scott, Sir Walter, 69, 141
Screening Byron,
     (Ralston/Sondergard), 150–151
Scriptores Graeci, 18, 23
"She Walks in Beauty," 59, 70, 86
     theme, 87
Shelley, Percy Bysshe, 45, 72, 74, 81,
     85, 100
     death of, 50–51
Siege of Corinth, The, 90, 96
Siege of Ismail, 122–123
Silver-fork novels, 148
Six Mile Bottom, 40–41, 69
     Augusta's home, 36
Smith, Constance Spencer, 26, 29
Smyrna, 28
Sodergard, 150
Soderholm, James, 144, 146
"So We'll Go No More A Roving," 47
Spain, 25–26
"Spirit Passed Before Me, A," 91
"Stanzas for Music," 98–99
Sterling, Bruce, 132
Stoppard, Tom, 144, 149–150
Strickland, Margot, 32, 40
     on Byron's disturbing ideas, 43
Suarez, Ganzalo, 150
Suliotes, 54–56
"Sun of the Sleepless," 71
Swineburne, 152
Symons, Arthur, 143–144

Tasso's cell, 78
Tennyson, 85

"There's Not a Joy," 100
Thorslev, Peter L., 137
"Thy Days are Done," 89
"Thyrza, To," 30
Tom Jones, (Fielding), 80–81
Tories, 24, 30, 43
Tory Riot Bill, 30
Turkey, 26
Turkish History, (Knolle), 9

Undead Byron, (essay), Holland, 145

Vampyre, The, (Polidori), 145–146
Venetia, (Disraeli), 147
Vision of Judgement, 50, 96

Wain, John, 6, 11
     and Byron's title, 10
"Waltz, The," 35
Whale, James, 150
"When Coldness Wraps This
     Suffering Clay," 91–93
Whigs, 21, 24, 30, 43
"Wild Gazelle, The," 88
William the Conqueror, 6
Willis, Karen
     Biography of Lord Byron, 5–58
Wilson, Andy, 151
Wilson, Frances
     biographical info, 152–155
     Byron, Byronism, and Byromaniacs,
     131–152
Woolf, Virginia, 149
Wordsworth, 81, 135–136, 144, 149
Wuthering Heights, (Bronte), 62

Yeats, William B., 72

Zeluco, (Moore), 9